Series/Number 07–146

LOGISTIC REGRESSION MODELS FOR ORDINAL RESPONSE VARIABLES

ANN A. O'CONNELL
University of Connecticut

SAGE PUBLICATIONS
International Educational and Professional Publisher
Thousand Oaks   London   New Delhi

For information:

Sage Publications, Inc.
2455 Teller Road
Thousand Oaks, California 91320
E-mail: order@sagepub.com

Sage Publications Ltd.
1 Oliver's Yard
55 City Road
London EC1Y 1SP
United Kingdom

Sage Publications India Pvt. Ltd.
B-42, Panchsheel Enclave
Post Box 4109
New Delhi 110 017 India

Printed in the United States of America

Library of Congress Cataloging-in-Publication Data

O'Connell, Ann A.
Logistic regression models for ordinal response variables / Ann A. O'Connell.
    p. cm. — (Quantitative applications in the social sciences; no. 146)
Includes bibliographical references and index.
ISBN 978-0-7619-2989-5 (pbk.)
    1. Logistic regression analysis. 2. Social sciences—Statistical methods. 3. Educational statistics. I. Title. II. Series: Sage university papers series. Quantitative applications in the social sciences; no. 146.
HA31.3.O27 2006
519.5'36—dc22

This book is printed on acid-free paper.

10   11   12   10 9 8 7 6 5 4 3 2

Acquisitions Editor:	Lisa Cuevas Shaw
Editorial Assistant:	Karen Gia Wong
Production Editor:	Melanie Birdsall
Copy Editor:	A. J. Sobczak
Typesetter:	C&M Digitals (P) Ltd.
Indexer:	Sheila Bodell

For Nathan, and especially for Delaney

CONTENTS

LIST OF TABLES AND FIGURES

Tables

Figures

SERIES EDITOR'S INTRODUCTION

Over the past three decades, logit type models have become the most popular statistical methods in the social sciences. In response to the need for understanding such models and showing how to correctly use them in various contexts, the Sage QASS (Quantitative Applications in the Social Sciences) series has given considerable attention to their exposition: The coverage includes No. 45 in the series, *Linear Probability, Logit, and Probit Models*, by Aldrich and Nelson; No. 86, *Logit Modeling*, by DeMaris; No. 101, *Interpreting Probability Models: Logit, Probit, and Other Generalized Linear Models*, by Liao; No. 106, *Applied Logistic Regression*, by Menard; No. 132, *Logistic Regression: A Primer*, by Pampel; No. 134, *Generalized Linear Models: A Unified Approach*, by Gill; No. 135, *Interaction Effects in Logistic Regression*, by Jaccard; and No. 138, *Logit and Probit: Ordered and Multinomial Models*, by Borooah. Why did my predecessor, Michael Lewis-Beck, who reviewed the prospectus and earlier drafts, put in the good work of editing another book on logit models for the series?

Since Rensis Likert's 1932 publication of *A Technique for the Measurement of Attitudes*, surveying human attitudes has never been the same. Indeed, any social surveys today will include the Likert-type scale as a staple means for asking questions. A typical Likert-type scale has five categories (e.g., *strongly disagree, disagree, undecided, agree, strongly agree*) to gauge one's response to a question, though it may have anywhere between three and seven or more response categories. If we code the five categories 1 to 5, we could estimate a linear regression model of a Likert-type scale, and that was the choice of method in the early days for analyzing such data. There are, however, some obvious problems. First and foremost, classical linear regression assumes a continuous dependent variable with equally spaced, ordered response categories. A Likert-type scale, or any other ordinal scale, is, albeit ordered, not necessarily equally spaced between categories. Second, and perhaps more important, such a scale would not give the normal distribution that the classical linear regression assumes the data to display.

To analyze ordinal data of this nature, there are other methods available, most often in the form of contingency tables and log-linear models. The Sage QASS series has also given attention to the topic, with the titles related to the topic including: No. 8, *Analysis of Ordinal Data*, by Hildebrand, Laing, and Rosenthal; No. 20, *Log-Linear Models*, by Knoke and Burke; No. 94, *Loglinear Models With Latent Variables*, by Hagenaars; No. 97, *Ordinal Log-Linear Models*, by Ishii-Kuntz; and No. 119, *Odds Ratios in the Analysis of Contingency Tables*, by Rudas. However, these methods are not in the regression framework, which is the most widely known and applied quantitative method in the social sciences.

Ann A. O'Connell's book fills the void. Even though Nos. 86, 101, and 138 in the series also treat ordered response variable in a logit model, the current book focuses entirely on such logit models by presenting three forms of the dependent variables that capture the ordinal nature of the response. The book begins by presenting an empirical example from the Early Childhood Longitudinal Study, for which the main dependent variable, although not a Likert scale, is nevertheless ordinal and measures proficiency in early literacy and numeracy. The author then reviews the logistic regression before presenting the core of the book in three topical chapters on the cumulative or proportional odds model, the continuation ratio model, and the adjacent categories model. Along the way, SAS® and SPSS® examples are given. Although the proportional odds model is perhaps the more widely applied of the three, the reader will appreciate the alternatives and especially the tips on when to use which, given in the concluding chapter.

—*Tim Futing Liao*
Series Editor

ACKNOWLEDGMENTS

Special thanks to Rosemarie L. Ataya for her initial and ongoing encouragement during the writing of this book, to D. Betsy McCoach for reading and rereading many drafts, and to several of my graduate students for their work on tables and some of the analyses: Heather Levitt Doucette, Jessica Goldstein, and Xing Liu. I would also like to thank John Fox, Scott Menard, and Timothy McDaniel for their reviews and valuable comments and suggestions, all of which greatly improved my own thinking and the quality of this work.

This research was supported in part by a grant from the American Educational Research Association, which receives funds for its "AERA Grants Program" from the National Science Foundation and the U.S. Department of Education's National Center for Education Statistics and the Office of Educational Research and Improvement (now the Institute for Education Sciences), under NSF Grant #REC-9980573. Opinions reflect those of the author and do not necessarily reflect those of the granting agencies.

LOGISTIC REGRESSION MODELS FOR ORDINAL RESPONSE VARIABLES

Ann A. O'Connell
University of Connecticut

1. INTRODUCTION

For many response variables in education and the social sciences, ordinal scales provide a simple and convenient way to distinguish between possible outcomes that can best be considered as rank-ordered. The primary characteristic of ordinal data is that the numbers assigned to successive categories of the variable being measured represent differences in magnitude, or a "greater than" or "less than" quality (Stevens, 1946, 1951). Some examples of ordinal data include rubrics for scaling open-ended writing responses or essays and the solutions to arithmetic problems for which responses are scored based on improving levels of quality (e.g., 0 = poor, 1 = acceptable, 2 = excellent). In contrast, nominal-level data occur when the numeric values used to measure a variable simply identify distinct qualitative differences between categories (i.e., gender as 1 = male or 2 = female; geographic description of school attended as 1 = rural, 2 = urban, 3 = suburban, etc.); nominal data do not possess the directional characteristics of ordinal data. On the other hand, variables measured on an interval-level or ratio-level scale do use scale values to indicate the "greater than" or "less than" quality of ordinal variables but in addition maintain a property of equal-distance or equal-interval length between adjacent values across the scale. Temperature measured on the Celsius scale is a familiar example of an interval-level variable. However, interval-level variables have an arbitrary rather than an absolute zero-point. Variables that possess all the properties of interval scales but that also have a genuine zero-point are referred to as ratio-level; reaction time to a task, weight, and distance are familiar ratio-level variables.[1]

Ordinal categories are common in research situations where the assignment of numbers representing successive categories of an attribute, construct, or behavior coincides with meaningful directional differences. Knapp (1999) used ordinal ratings to assess severity of illness with scale categories such as mild (1), moderate (2), and severe (3). In Knapp's research, the numbers ascribed to the severity of illness categories represent increasing severity, in the sense that "moderate" is more critical than "mild," and "severe" is more critical than "moderate." The numerical rating given to the "severe" case does not imply that "severe" is three times as critical than "mild," only that the severity of illness in the "severe" category is greater than the severity of illness for those in the "mild" category, and greater still than those in the "moderate" category.

The choice of numbers used to represent the progressively more severe categories conveniently preserves the "greater than" or "less than" quality of the underlying attribute defining the categories themselves. The numbers model the attribute under study, such as severity of illness, and are chosen to preserve the transitivity of the categories: If the value of 3 represents a state that is more critical than the state represented by the value 2, and the value 2 represents a state more critical than the condition represented by the value 1, then the property of transitivity implies that the condition represented by the value of 3 is also more critical than the condition represented by the value of 1 (Cliff & Keats, 2003; Krantz, Luce, Suppes, & Tversky, 1971).

The measurement of variables on an ordinal scale is familiar. Ordinal scales have been used to categorize subjective probability or likelihood judgments in counseling and psychotherapy research (e.g., ratings from 1 = *very unlikely* to 5 = *very likely*) (Ness, 1995). A client's clinical condition after therapy can be characterized as deteriorated (1), unchanged (2), or improved (3) (Grissom, 1994). Health researchers frequently use five successive levels to characterize "stages of change" in health-related behavior such as smoking cessation, use of condoms, exercise behavior, and weight loss efforts (Hedeker & Mermelstein, 1998; Plotnikoff, Blanchard, Hotz, & Rhodes, 2001; Prochaska & DiClemente, 1983, 1986; Prochaska, DiClemente, & Norcross, 1992). In the stages-of-change model, disposition or activity toward behavior change typically is measured as precontemplation (1), contemplation (2), preparation (3), action (4), and maintenance (5). The experience of teachers' stages of concern for implementation of educational innovations in their classrooms has also been measured through an ordinal scale, one representing change in focus of concern from *self* = 1 to *other* = 7 (Hall & Hord, 1984; van den Berg, Sleegers, Geijsel, & Vandenberghe, 2000). In early-childhood education, indicators of mastery for the hierarchy of early literacy skills leading toward literacy proficiency in young children can be characterized as ordinal in nature: phonemic awareness (1), phonics (2), fluency (3), vocabulary (4), and text comprehension (5) (Center for the Improvement of Early Reading Achievement [CIERA], 2001).

Although ordinal outcomes can be simple and meaningful, their optimal statistical treatment remains challenging to many applied researchers (Cliff,

1996a; Clogg & Shihadeh, 1994; Ishii-Kuntz, 1994). Historically, researchers have relied on two very different approaches for the analysis of ordinal outcomes. Some researchers choose to apply parametric models for ordinal outcomes, such as through multiple linear regression with the outcome treated as at least an interval-level variable, assuming that the robustness of these techniques overcomes any potential interpretation problems. Other researchers choose to treat the ordinal variable as strictly categorical and apply log-linear or nonparametric approaches to understand the data. Although both strategies may be informative, depending on the research question, neither of these approaches is optimal for developing explanatory models of ordinal outcomes (Agresti, 1989; Cliff, 1996a; Clogg & Shihadeh, 1994; O'Connell, 2000), particularly when the focus of analysis is on the distinction between the ordinal scores.

Purpose of This Book

The purpose of this book is to familiarize applied researchers, particularly those within the fields of education and social and behavioral science, with alternatives for the analysis of ordinal response variables that are faithful to the actual level of measure of the outcome. The methods I discuss are examples of ordinal regression models, and they are extensions to logistic models for binary response data. Logistic regression methods are firmly established within epidemiology, medicine, and related fields, and in fact, much of the recent literature on application and development of ordinal regression techniques is found within the research of the larger public health community. Results of many of these statistical or comparative studies are mentioned here. Educational and social scientists may not typically focus on variables similar to those studied by epidemiologists or medical researchers, but both fields struggle with issues surrounding the aptness of models, and much can be learned about applications of different approaches to statistical dilemmas from the broader statistical literature.

In this book, three different methods for analyzing ordinal outcome data will be reviewed and illustrated through examples. These include the proportional or cumulative odds model (CO) (Agresti, 1996; Armstrong & Sloan, 1989; Long, 1997; McCullagh, 1980), the continuation ratio model (CR) (Armstrong & Sloan, 1989; D. R. Cox, 1972; Greenland, 1994), and the adjacent categories model (AC) (Agresti, 1989; Goodman, 1983). In addition, I present examples of partial proportional odds (Peterson & Harrell, 1990) and discuss the partial proportional hazards or unconstrained continuation ratio models (Bender & Benner, 2000; Cole & Ananth, 2001) as analysis alternatives for situations in which assumptions of the proportional odds or continuation ratio model are violated.

Ordinal logit models can be viewed as extensions of logistic regression for dichotomous outcomes, and consequently these models closely follow the approaches and model building strategies of both logistic and ordinary least squares regression analysis. I have chosen to focus on logit models for ordinal outcomes because the interpretations of probability and odds that derive from these models are somewhat intuitive. Alternatives to the methods presented here include, for example, Anderson's (1984) stereotype model, probit regression models, and the use of polychoric correlations for structural equation modeling of ordinal outcome variables. These and other strategies for analysis of ordinal data are discussed in Huynh (2002), Borooah (2002), Ishii-Kuntz (1994), Liao (1994), Menard (1995), and Jöreskog and Sörbom (1996); valuable references on the treatment of ordinal variables in general include Long (1997), Clogg and Shihadeh (1994), and Agresti (1989, 1996).

The cumulative odds model is the most frequently used ordinal regression model, although all of the models examined here are still relatively unfamiliar to many applied researchers, particularly in the educational sciences. Each of the models I review can address questions that are unique to the study of ordinal outcomes and that may not be satisfactorily answered by treating the data as either interval/ratio or strictly categorical.

Software and Syntax

The SAS® and SPSS® software packages are used for the examples presented here. Within each of these statistical packages, I used SAS PROC LOGISTIC (ascending and descending options), SAS PROC GENMOD, SAS PROC CATMOD, SPSS LOGISTIC REGRESSION, and SPSS PLUM to run the different models. Appendices in this book include the syntax used for each analysis presented, and both this syntax and the data can be found at my Web site (http://faculty.education.uconn.edu/epsy/aoconnell/index .htm). Limitations of, as well as similarities and differences between, the statistical packages will be noted as needed throughout this book. All analyses presented here assume independence across children. In the final chapter of this book, I briefly discuss the treatment of ordinal response variables for multilevel data, a rapidly building field that logically extends from work on the proportional odds model for single-level data and the fitting of multilevel models in general.

I focus on SAS and SPSS to illustrate the concepts and procedures for ordinal logit models included in this book. Another comprehensive statistical package for the analysis of categorical data in general, one that contains excellent modules for analysis of ordinal data, is Stata (Long & Freese, 2003). Stata also includes graphical capabilities that can facilitate further understanding of the models presented here. The descriptions of the models included in this book are appropriate regardless of choice of statistical package.

Organization of the Chapters

Chapter 2 describes the data set used for the analyses presented here. Chapter 3 includes a brief review of logistic regression analysis, clarifying terminology important to the understanding of logit type ordinal regression models including odds, odd ratios, logits, and model fit. Each of the three ordinal models (CO, CR, AC) will then be described and illustrated in Chapters 4–6, building on their conceptual similarity to logistic regression models. For each of the ordinal models presented, model and variable effects will be explained, and assessment of model fit and predictive efficiency will be discussed. Chapter 4 provides a comparison with ordinary least squares multiple regression. Finally, Chapter 7 reviews and summarizes the analyses studied here and discusses some extensions to these models. Selected computer output will be included for each of the analyses presented.

The data for the examples contained in this book were drawn from the Early Childhood Longitudinal Study-Kindergarten Cohort (ECLS-K), which tracks the reading and arithmetic progress of a nationally representative sample of kindergarten children through the completion of first grade (third-grade data were released in March, 2004). Data from first-grade entry are analyzed here. The ECLS-K is conducted by the U.S. National Center for Education Statistics (NCES) and, in part, assesses student proficiency for early literacy, mathematics, and general knowledge as a series of "stepping-stones," which reflect the ordinal skills that form the foundation for further learning (West, Denton, & Germino-Hausken, 2000). All of the data are available on the first-grade public-use databases that can be obtained from NCES.[2] The examples illustrated here were derived solely for the purpose of explicating the technical and methodological use of ordinal regression models; although they are informative, they are not meant to provide a complete picture of early reading achievement for first-grade children. See, for example, Snow, Burns, and Griffin (1998) for further information about factors affecting early-childhood reading.

2. CONTEXT: EARLY CHILDHOOD LONGITUDINAL STUDY

Overview of the Early Childhood Longitudinal Study

The Early Childhood Longitudinal Study provides a comprehensive picture of first-grade children, their kindergarten and early home experiences, their teachers, and their schools. The ECLS-K investigates early literacy, reading, and arithmetic skills. It includes a battery of IRT (item-response theory)-scaled cognitive assessments collected on a nationally representative sample of approximately 20,000 children within sampled schools. In addition to the norm-referenced continuous IRT measures, the ECLS-K assesses criterion-referenced student proficiency for literacy and numeracy through responses to a series of five 4-item clusters that, as a set, reflect the skills that serve as stepping-stones for subsequent learning in reading and mathematics. The resulting scores can be used individually for student-level diagnosis and to identify directions for individualized interventions, as well as being used at a group level to suggest possible interventions for groups of students functioning at different levels of mastery. The analyses discussed in this book will focus on the criterion-referenced scores for literacy proficiency.

The categorization of early literacy proficiencies represented in the ECLS-K assessment instrument is consistent with the skills that have been identified as the building blocks of reading mastery: *phonemic awareness* (the understanding that letters represent spoken sounds), *phonics* (understanding the sounds of letters in combination), *fluency*, *vocabulary*, and *text comprehension* (CIERA, 2001). The skills underlying literacy development are hierarchical and interdependent; the later skills cannot realistically be expected to emerge without the development of the former. Table 2.1 describes the proficiency categories utilized by the ECLS-K.

The ability to respond sufficiently to the cluster of items represented by each category is assumed to follow the Guttman model (Guttman, 1954; NCES, 2000, 2002); that is, mastery at one level assumes mastery at all previous levels. On the ECLS-K assessments, a pass/fail score was obtained for each child in the sample on each cluster of items representing a proficiency level (1 through 5) until the child failed to pass three out of the four items in a cluster.[3] Mastery of one cluster indicates mastery of all previous clusters; testing was stopped once a child was unable to successfully pass a cluster of items.[4] Consequently, there are five dichotomous variables for literacy proficiency (C3RRPRF1 to C3RRPRF5) in the ECLS-K database. For example, if a child passes three out of four items in literacy level 1 and

TABLE 2.1
Proficiency Categories for the ECLS-K
Measures for Early Literacy

Proficiency Category	Description
0	Did not pass level 1
1	Can identify upper/lowercase letters
2	Can associate letters with sounds at the beginnings of words
3	Can associate letters with sounds at the ends of words
4	Can recognize sight words
5	Can read words in context

SOURCE: National Center for Education Statistics (2002).

three out of four items in literacy level 2, that child would receive a value of 1 for both C3RRPRF1 and C3RRPRF2. If this same child does not pass three out of four items in the next cluster (literacy level 3), a score of 0 is recorded for C3RRPRF3 as well as for all subsequent levels. For the analyses presented here, the series of five dichotomous proficiency values was used to create a single variable that reflects mastery of the content areas on an ordinal scale. After recoding to achieve a single ordinal variable, the hypothetical student above would receive a value of 2 as his or her proficiency score, representing mastery of material up to and including level 2. In this manner, a single variable (*profread*) with six possible outcome categories (levels 0 through 5) for the assessment of literacy proficiency was derived for each child in the ECLS-K sample. A score of 0 on this ordinal scale implies that the child did not attain mastery for the cluster of items representing proficiency level 1.[5]

Practical Relevance of Ordinal Outcomes

Ordinal proficiency scores can reveal to researchers and educators how far along children are on the path to becoming fully literate as they continue through their primary school education. Analyzing the ordinal proficiency scores rather than the continuous IRT-scaled scores as the variables of interest highlights the role that proficiency assessments can play in the identification and selection of students for early intervention programs. These analyses can suggest concrete areas in the hierarchy where interventions might be tailored to meet particular student needs. Ordinal proficiency outcomes, and indeed ordinal variables in general, have a great deal of pragmatic utility in the degree to which they can direct intervention to specific levels of proficiency. For the classroom teacher or reading specialist, proficiency scores may be far more valuable, and interpretable, than knowing that a child's IRT-scaled score on a cognitive assessment is "55." Interventions tailored to the classroom, or school practices or policies found to be associated with the stepping-stones to successful acquisition of literacy skills, may be far more effective for individual students than strategies based on attempts to improve a global cognitive test score (obtained at the classroom, school, or district level).

Variables in the Models

The variables selected as predictors in the analyses presented here have been found to be associated with early reading skill among young children. Initial data summaries of the ECLS kindergarten cohort indicate that some children do enter kindergarten with greater preparedness and "readiness" to learn than that exhibited by other children, perhaps putting them a step ahead of their peers for the important early grades at school (NCES, 2000). ECLS-K studies have shown that children entering kindergarten who have particular characteristics (living in a single-parent household, living in a family that receives welfare payments or food stamps, having a mother with less than a high school education, or having parents whose primary language is not English) tended to be at risk for low reading skills (Zill & West, 2001). Pre-kindergarten experiences related to family life (e.g., being read to by parents), attendance at preschool or day care, and personal characteristics (e.g., gender) may relate to children's initial proficiency in reading as well as to their potential growth in skills and abilities across the kindergarten year and beyond. For example, girls typically enter kindergarten with slightly greater early literacy ability than boys. Child-focused predictors of success and failure in early reading are helpful for understanding how individual children may be at risk for reading difficulties. From a policy and practice perspective, it is clearly desirable that teachers, school administrators, parents, and other stakeholders be aware of these individual factors related to early proficiency so that these stakeholders can develop and support curriculum and instructional practices that can promote achievement for all students relative to their first-grade and kindergarten entry skills.

Descriptive statistics for the explanatory variables across the six proficiency categories are presented in Table 2.2. These include *gender*, shown here as % *male* (0 = female, 1 = male), *risknum* (number of family risk characteristics, ranging from 0 to 4, based on parent characteristics including living in a single-parent household, living in a family that receives welfare payments or food stamps, having a mother with less than a high school education, or having parents whose primary language is not English), *famrisk* (dichotomous variable indicating whether or not any family risk was present, coded 0 = no, 1 = yes [or *risknum* greater than or equal to 1]), *p1readbo* (frequency with which parents read books to children prior to kindergarten entry, rated as 1 to 4 with 1 = never and 4 = every day), *noreadbo* (dichotomized variable indicating 0 = parent reads books to child three or more times a week to every day and 1 = parent reads books to child less than once or twice per week), *halfdayK* (child attended half-day versus full-day kindergarten, coded 0 = no [attended full-day K], 1 = yes [attended half-day K]), *center* (whether or not child ever received center-based day care prior to attending kindergarten; 0 = no, 1 = yes), *minority* (0 = white/Caucasian background; 1 = minority [any other] background), *wksesl* (family SES assessed prior to kindergarten entry, continuous scaled score with mean of 0), and *p1ageent* (age of child in months at kindergarten entry). An additional variable, included for descriptive purposes but not included in the models because of design concerns, is *public* (type of school child attended, rated as 0 = private, 1 = public).

TABLE 2.2
Descriptive Statistics at First-Grade Entry, $N = 3,365$

	Reading Proficiency Level (profread)						
	0 (n = 67)	*1* (n = 278)	*2* (n = 594)	*3* (n = 1,482)	*4* (n = 587)	*5* (n = 357)	*Total* (N = 3,365)
% profread	2.0%	8.3%	17.7%	44.0%	17.4%	10.6%	100%
% male	71.6%	58.6%	53.9%	49.6%	43.6%	42.3%	49.7%
risknum							
M	.97	.77	.65	.44	.32	.25	.47
(SD)	(1.04)	(0.88)	(0.88)	(0.71)	(0.61)	(0.53)	(0.75)
% famrisk	58.2%	52.9%	43.8%	32.5%	25.9%	20.7%	34.3%
% noreadbo	38.8%	27.0%	21.7%	15.5%	13.1%	7.6%	16.7%
% halfdayK	43.3%	41.7%	46.3%	48.0%	40.7%	43.7%	45.3%
% center	71.6%	73.7%	71.0%	77.5%	78.7%	84.9%	76.9%
% minority	59.7%	58.3%	48.5%	33.3%	34.2%	33.9%	38.8%
wksesl							
M	−.6133	−.2705	−.1234	.1490	.2807	.6148	.1235
(SD)	(0.67)	(0.64)	(0.71)	(0.75)	(0.70)	(0.75)	(0.76)
p1ageent							
M	65.6	65.1	65.5	66.1	66.5	67.1	66.1
(SD)	(4.40)	(4.34)	(3.97)	(4.00)	(4.07)	(3.86)	(4.06)
% public	98.5%	93.5%	86.9%	76.7%	70.9%	61.9%	77.7%

The design of the ECLS-K sampling plan called for oversampling of children with Asian and Pacific Islander backgrounds, and it currently includes three waves of data, collected at kindergarten entry, at the end of the kindergarten year, and at the end of the first-grade year. Third-grade data were released in the spring of 2004. Data also were collected on a 30% subsample of children at first-grade entry. All data used for the examples presented here were contained in the 30% first-grade subsample; the children had no missing data on the variables of interest, were first-time kindergarteners (no repeaters), and remained in the same school for first grade that they attended in kindergarten. Given the focus of this book and the oversampling of Asian/Pacific Islanders, coupled with sparse cells for other minority groups, a dichotomous variable for race/ethnicity was created with a classification of 1 = minority group and 0 = white/Caucasian for these illustrative models. With this criteria, there were $n = 3,365$ children from 255 schools (57 private and 198 public), with an average of 13 students per school. Incorporating the nested design into the analysis of ordinal outcome data is addressed in Chapter 7; all other analyses assume independence of children across schools.

3. BACKGROUND: LOGISTIC REGRESSION

Overview of Logistic Regression

Ordinal regression models are closely related to logistic models for dichotomous outcomes, so I begin with a brief review of logistic regression analysis in order to highlight similarities and differences in later chapters. Other authors in the QASS series and elsewhere (e.g., Cizek & Fitzgerald, 1999; Hosmer & Lemeshow, 1989, 2000; Menard, 1995, 2000; Pampel, 2000) have covered logistic regression in depth, so only those concepts important to the discussion later in this book are included here.

The terminology and estimation strategies for fitting ordinal regression models are fairly straightforward extensions of those used for logistic regression. These models are collectively defined as a class of generalized linear models, consisting of three components:

- A random component, where the dependent variable Y follows one of the distributions from the exponential family such as the normal, binomial, or inverse Gaussian

- A linear component, which describes how a function, Y', of the dependent variable Y depends on a collection of predictors
- A link function, which describes the transformation of the dependent variable Y to Y' (Fox, 1997).

The identity link function does not alter the dependent variable, leading to the general linear model for continuous outcomes, for which multiple linear regression is the familiar case. The logit link function transforms the outcome variable to the natural log of the odds (explained below), which leads to the logistic regression model.

Logistic analyses for binary outcomes attempt to model the odds of an event's occurrence and to estimate the effects of independent variables on these odds. The odds for an event is a quotient that conveniently compares the probability that an event occurs (referred to as "success") to the probability that it does not occur (referred to as "failure," or the complement of success). When the probability of success is greater than the probability of failure, the odds are greater than 1.0; if the two outcomes are equally likely, the odds are 1.0; and if the probability of success is less than the probability of failure, the odds are less than 1.0.

For the ECLS-K example described above, suppose we are interested in studying the attainment of reading proficiency category 5 (sight words) among children at first-grade entry. The outcome can be described as binary: A child attains proficiency in category 5 (success) or not (failure). The odds of reaching category 5 are computed from the sample data by dividing the probability of reaching category 5 (scored as $Y = 1$) by the probability of not reaching category 5 (scored as $Y = 0$):

$$\text{Odds} = \frac{P(Y = 1)}{P(Y = 0)} = \frac{P(Y = 1)}{1 - P(Y = 1)}.$$

To examine the impact on the odds of an independent variable, such as gender or age, we construct the odds ratio (OR), which compares the odds for different values of the explanatory variable. For example, if we want to compare the odds of reaching proficiency category 5 between males (coded $x = 1$) and females (coded $x = 0$), we would compute the following ratio:

$$OR = \frac{\dfrac{P(Y = 1|x = 1)}{1 - P(Y = 1|x = 1)}}{\dfrac{P(Y = 1|x = 0)}{1 - P(Y = 1|x = 0)}}.$$

Odds ratios are bounded below by 0 but have no upper bound; that is, they can range from 0 to infinity. An OR of 1.0 indicates that an explanatory variable has no effect on the odds of success; that is, the odds of success for males is the same as the odds of success for females. Small values of the OR (< 1.0) indicate that the odds of success for the persons with the value of x used in the denominator (0 = females) are greater than the odds of success for the persons with the higher value of x used in the numerator (1 = males). The opposite is true for values of the OR that exceed 1.0; that is that the odds for males of being in proficiency category 5 is greater than the odds for females. The nature and type of coding used for the independent variables become important in interpretation; in this example and throughout this text, I used simple dummy or referent coding. Other approaches to coding categorical independent variables can change the interpretation of that variable's effect in the model; discussions of alternative approaches to categorizing qualitative data in logistic regression models can be found in Hosmer and Lemeshow (2000).

The OR is a measure of association between the binary outcome and an independent variable that provides "a clear indication of how the risk of the outcome being present changes with the variable in question" (Hosmer & Lemeshow, 1989, p. 57). Although the probability of an event could be modeled directly through the linear probability model (i.e., using ordinary linear regression on the dichotomous [0, 1] dependent variable), such an approach leads to some serious interpretation problems. The linear probability model can yield implausible predictions outside the 0, 1 bounds for probability, particularly if the independent variable is continuous. In addition, the typical assumptions of homoscedasticity and normality of errors from the ordinary linear regression model are violated when the outcome is dichotomous, calling the validity of results from such an approach into question (Cizek & Fitzgerald, 1999; Ishii-Kuntz, 1994; O'Connell, 2000). Instead, when the outcome is dichotomous, we model the odds, or more specifically, we model the natural (base e) log of the odds, referred to as the *logit* of a distribution.

This simple transformation of the odds has many desirable properties. First, it eliminates the skewness inherent in estimates of the OR (Agresti, 1996), which can range from 0 to infinity, with a value of 1.0 indicating the *null* case of *no change in the odds*. The logit ranges from negative infinity to infinity, which eliminates the boundary problems of both the OR and probability. The transformed model is linear in the parameters, which means that the effects of explanatory variables on the log of the odds are additive. Thus, the model is easy to work with and allows for interpretation of variable effects that are exceptionally straightforward, and for model-building strategies that mirror those of ordinary linear regression.

This process can be extended to include more than one independent variable. If we let $\pi(Y = 1|X_1, X_2, \ldots X_p) = \pi(\underline{x})$ represent the probability of "success," or the outcome of interest (e.g., a child being in proficiency category 5), for a given set of p independent variables, then the logistic model can be written as

$$\ln(Y') = \text{logit}\,[\pi(\underline{x})] = \ln\left(\frac{\pi(\underline{x})}{1 - \pi(\underline{x})}\right)$$

$$= \alpha + \beta_1 X_1 + \beta_2 X_2 + \ldots \beta_p X_p.$$

In this expression, Y' is simply a convenient way to refer to the odds in the transformed outcome variable; rather than predicting Y directly, we are predicting the (log of the) odds of $Y = 1$. The link function describes the process of "linking" the original Y to the transformed outcome: $f(y) = \ln(Y')$ $= \ln[\pi(\underline{x})/(1 - \pi(\underline{x}))]$, which is referred to as the logit link. Solving for $\pi(\underline{x})$ gives us the familiar expression for the logistic regression model for the probability of success:

$$\pi(\underline{x}) = \frac{\exp(\alpha + \beta_1 X_1 + \beta_2 X_2 + \ldots \beta_p X_p)}{1 + \exp(\alpha + \beta_1 X_1 + \beta_2 X_2 + \ldots \beta_p X_p)}$$

$$= \frac{1}{1 + \exp[-(\alpha + \beta_1 X_1 + \beta_2 X_2 + \ldots \beta_p X_p)]}.$$

Statistical packages such as SPSS and SAS provide maximum likelihood (ML) estimates of the intercept and regression weights for the variables in the model. Maximum likelihood estimates are derived using an iterative method that returns the "values for the population parameters that 'best' explain the observed data" (Johnson & Wichern, 1998, p. 178). These ML estimates maximize the likelihood of obtaining the original data, and because the logistic model is developed through a nonlinear transformation of the outcome, the method does not require a normal distribution of the error terms, as does ordinary least squares estimation. The likelihood represents the probability that the observed outcomes can be predicted from the set of independent variables. Likelihood can vary between 0 and 1; the log-likelihood (LL) varies from negative infinity to 0. Multiplying the LL by –2 creates a quantity that can be used for hypothesis testing purposes to compare different models (Hosmer & Lemeshow, 2000).

Assessing Model Fit

One way to assess how well a fitted model reproduces the observed data is to compute the "deviance" for the fitted model. The deviance represents how *poorly* the model reproduces the observed data, and it is found by comparing the likelihood of the fitted model to a model that has a perfect fit, called the saturated model.[6] The saturated model has as many parameters as there are values of the independent variable; the likelihood of the saturated model is 1.0, and $-2LL$(saturated model) $= 0$. The "deviance" of any model, D_m, is thus the quantity $-2LL$ (see Hosmer & Lemeshow, 2000). We would expect the "poorness" of fit to decrease (toward 0) with better-fitting models. The fit of two nested models, with variables in Model 1 a subset of those in Model 2, can be compared by considering the difference of their deviances: $G = D_{m1} - D_{m2}$. The quantity G represents "goodness" of fit, and for large samples, G follows an approximate chi-square distribution with degrees of freedom equal to the difference in number of parameters estimated between Model 1 and Model 2. A statistically significant G indicates that Model 2 has less "poorness" of fit than Model 1.

When Model 1 is the null model, this comparison provides an omnibus test (assuming large-sample properties and non-sparse cells) for whether or not the fitted model reproduces the observed data better than the null, or intercept only, model. However, it does not tell us how well the model performs relative to the saturated, or perfect, model. With categorical predictors, SAS tests D_m (which compares the fitted to the saturated model) using the Pearson χ^2 criteria or the Deviance χ^2 criteria. Neither of these is appropriate when continuous explanatory variables are included (see Allison, 1999; Hosmer & Lemeshow, 2000). When explanatory variables are categorical, these tests can be generated in SAS using the "*/aggregate scale=none*" option in the model statement.

With small samples or when sparse cells are present in the data (which nearly always will occur with the inclusion of continuous independent variables in the model), alternative methods for assessing model fit should be considered; a common strategy is known as the Hosmer-Lemeshow (H-L) test (1989, 2000). The H-L test is obtained through SAS by requesting the "*/lackfit*" option in the model statement; in SPSS, the test is provided when "*goodfit*" is included in the print statement.

The H-L test works well when independent variables (IVs) are continuous, because it deals directly with the number of covariate patterns within the data. When IVs are continuous, there is essentially a different possible covariate pattern for each observation in the data set. Briefly, the H-L test forms several groups referred to as "deciles of risk" based on the estimated probabilities for the sample. In most situations, g = 10 groups are formed, but there may be fewer depending on similarity of estimated probabilities across different covariate patterns. The cases within these deciles are then used to create a g × 2 table of observed to expected frequencies, and a Pearson χ^2 statistic is calculated for this table (Hosmer & Lemeshow, 1989, 2000). If the model fits well, agreement is expected between the observed and expected frequencies, so that the null hypothesis of a good fit between observed and expected frequencies from the model would be retained. The H-L test has been criticized in the literature for lack of power (Allison, 1999; Demaris, 1992), but reliance on a single test to indicate model adequacy is in itself discouraged (Hosmer & Lemeshow, 2000).[7] Supplemental strategies include measures of association and predicative efficiency, discussed later in this chapter.

Interpreting the Model

Typically, SPSS models the log of the odds for the dependent variable coded with the higher value (the 1, if the outcome is coded as 0 or 1), but SAS by default models the response coded with the lower value. With binary outcomes, the interpretation of results and effects of independent variables on the odds is not affected by decisions of how "success" versus "failure" are coded, because these two events are complements of each other. For example, let the probability of "success" as defined by P(reaching proficiency category 5) = .2. Then, the probability of "failure" or P(not reaching proficiency category 5) = 1 − .2 = .8. The odds of success would then be .25 (.2/.8). The odds for the complement of the event, which is not reaching proficiency category 5, would be 1/.25 or 4.0 (.8/.2). Because there are only two possible outcomes for the dependent variable, the odds for the complement of an event is simply the inverse of the odds for that event. When the logistic transformation is applied, we see that taking the log of the odds of an event $(\ln(.25) = -1.3863)$ has the opposite sign, but the same magnitude, of the log of the odds for the complement of the event $(\ln(4) = +1.3863)$. In the logistic regression model, reversing the coding for the outcome being modeled amounts to the same probability predictions and interpretations once the direction of the regression coefficients and the intercept are taken into account. With dichotomous outcomes, use of the "descending" option in the model statement for SAS changes the default approach and asks the computer to model the odds for the higher-valued outcome category, which would be the category labeled $Y = 1$ if the outcomes are coded as 0 or 1 (or category 2 if the outcomes are labeled as 1 and 2). However, with more than two *ordinal* response categories, applying the "descending" option can change the model dramatically and must be used with care. Use of this option for ordinal outcomes will be explained fully in Chapter 4.

For $j = 1$ to p independent variables, the regression weights in the multivariate logistic model represent the *change in the logit* for each one-unit increase in X_j, controlling or adjusting for the effects of the other independent variables in the model. Because it is more intuitive to consider variable effects in terms of the odds rather than the log-odds (the regression weights are in log-odds), information about the odds themselves is found by exponentiating the weights for the variables in the model (i.e., $\exp(b_j)$). The exponentiations of the regression weights are the ORs and are routinely reported in computer runs. The ORs can be interpreted directly to indicate the effect of an independent variable on the odds of success, and the percentage change in the odds also can be calculated using the following formula: $(100 \times [OR - 1])$.

Strong associations between independent variables and the outcome typically are represented by ORs farther from 1.0, in either direction. Long (1997) refers to the ORs as "factor change" estimates (p. 79). For a unit change in the independent variable, the corresponding OR is the factor by which the odds of "success" are expected to change, controlling for all other independent variables in the model. Statistical significance of an OR typically is assessed by testing if the regression coefficient, β_j, is statistically different from zero through one of three approaches: a Wald, score, or likelihood ratio test. In the Wald test, the parameter estimate for the effect of each independent variable in a logistic model is divided by its respective standard error, and the results are squared to represent a value from the chi-square distribution with one degree of freedom under the null hypothesis of no effect. However, the Wald statistics can be problematic in small samples; in samples with many different data patterns, such as when an independent variable is continuous rather than categorical; or in samples with sparse cells for categorical IVs (Jennings, 1986; Menard, 1995). Both SPSS and SAS report Wald chi-square statistics for each variable in the fitted model.

The score test for the contribution of an independent variable in the model relies on derivatives of the likelihood function and is not directly available in either SPSS or SAS; however, SPSS does use a score test in stepwise procedures to determine when variables enter or exit a developing model (Hosmer & Lemeshow, 2000). The likelihood ratio test has been advocated as the most reliable test for contribution of an independent variable to a model, but it is not directly available in either SPSS or SAS. The test can be obtained easily through some simple but possibly time-consuming programming, and it involves comparing the deviances for nested models, that is, the deviance from a model that does not contain the independent variable of interest to the deviance of a model that does. The difference in deviances approximates a chi-square distribution with one degree of freedom. Because the focus of this book is on development and overall interpretation of ordinal models, I chose to rely on the Wald test for assessing effects of explanatory variables. However, researchers do need to be aware that alternatives to this test exist.

Measures of Association

There are several logistic regression analogs to the familiar model R^2 from ordinary least squares regression that may be useful for informing about strength of association between the collection of independent variables and the outcome, although Menard (2000) and others (Borooah, 2002; Demaris, 1992; Long, 1997) point out that there is some disagreement among researchers as to which proportion reduction in error measure is most meaningful. For logit type models, the likelihood ratio R^2 value, R_L^2, seems to provide the most intuitive measure of improvement of fit for a multivariate model relative to the null (intercept only) model. R_L^2 is found by comparing two log-likelihoods: $R_L^2 = 1 - (\text{log-likelihood(model)}/\text{log-likelihood(null)})$ (Hosmer & Lemeshow, 2000; Long, 1997; McFadden, 1973; Menard, 2000). It measures the proportion reduction of error (log-likelihood) achieved from the use of the set of independent variables (relative to the null model). Other alternatives for measuring strength of association exist, but only a few will be discussed in the examples to follow. Long (1997) states that "While measures of fit provide some information, it is only partial information that must be assessed within the context of the theory motivating the analysis, past research, and the estimated parameters of the model being considered" (p. 102). The interested reader should consult Menard's (2000) discussion on the use of various R^2 analogs in logistic regression, as well as Borooah (2002, pp. 19–23). Huynh (2002) provides a discussion of extensions of these situations in which the outcome is ordinal rather than dichotomous.

EXAMPLE 3.1: Logistic Regression

A simple example will be used to illustrate the concepts above, as well as to provide an extension for developing an ordinal regression model. I chose a subset of the original ECLS-K data described above: $n = 702$ children who fell into proficiency categories 0, 1, or 5 when they were tested at the beginning of first grade. Table 3.1 provides the frequency breakdown for this subsample according to gender. The subsample is fairly balanced

TABLE 3.1
Cross-Tabulation of Proficiency (0, 1 versus 5) by Gender, $N = 702$

Gender	Y = 0 (profread category 0 or 1)	Y = 1 (profread category 5)	Totals
Males ($x = 1$)	211	151	362
Females ($x = 0$)	134	206	340
Totals	345	357	702

across the two outcomes. In the data analysis to follow, males were coded as "$x = 1$" and females as "$x = 0$," with the outcome of being in category 5 coded as "$Y = 1$" and being in either category 0 or 1 coded as "$Y = 0$."

The odds for a male being in the higher proficiency category can be found by dividing the probability of being in category 5 by the probability of not being in category 5:

$$\text{Odds (category 5|male)} = \frac{151/362}{211/362} = \frac{.4171}{1 - .4171} = .7156.$$

Similarly for females, the odds of being in proficiency category 5 are determined as

$$\text{Odds (category 5|female)} = \frac{206/340}{134/340} = \frac{.6059}{1 - .6059} = 1.537.$$

From these two values, we see that for this subsample, boys have a greater probability of being in categories 0 or 1 rather than in category 5 (the numerator is less than .5), and for girls, the opposite is true (the numerator is greater than .5). Thus, the odds for a boy of being in category 5 is less than the odds for a girl of being in category 5. The odds ratio (OR) compares these two odds and provides a measure of the association between gender and the odds of being in category 5:

$$\text{OR} = \frac{\text{Odds (category 5|male)}}{\text{Odds (category 5|female)}} = \frac{.7156}{1.537} = .466.$$

The OR of .466 informs us that, for this subsample, the odds for boys being in the higher proficiency category is .466 times the odds for girls of being in category 5, or less than half. Put another way, being a boy decreases the odds of being in category 5 by 53.4% (100 × [OR − 1] = −53.4). Conversely, the odds for a girl of being in category 5 is 2.146 times the odds for boys, or more than twice the odds for boys ($1/.466 = 2.146$).

In a logistic regression model, as discussed earlier, probability is transformed to the odds, and the odds are transformed to logits by taking the natural log. Selected output from fitting the logistic regression model for the above example using SPSS LOGISTIC REGRESSION is shown in Figure 3.1 (syntax in Appendix A, section A1). In this model, Y is coded 1 for being in proficiency category 5, and 0 if not. The explanatory variable, "*gender*," is coded 1 if the child is a boy, and 0 if the child is a girl. We will let $\ln(Y')$ represent the logit, or log-odds. The prediction model is $\ln(\hat{Y}') = .430 + (−.765)$ *gender*. Parameter estimates are found in the last section of Figure 3.1, "Variables in the Equation."

When the child is female (*gender* = 0), the constant represents the prediction for the log of the odds; it is .430. Exponentiating this back to the odds, we have $\exp(.430) = 1.537$, which is, as solved for above, the odds of being in proficiency category 5 for a girl. For boys (coded *gender* = 1), our model's prediction becomes $.430 + (−.765 × 1) = −.335$. Exponentiating this result, we have $\exp(−.335) = .7153$, which is (within rounding error) the odds of being in proficiency category 5 for a boy. Finally, the OR (taking rounding into consideration) can be found by exponentiating the regression weight for *gender*, $\exp(−.765) = .466$. This value appears in the final column of the "Variables in the Equation" table, and it is precisely the OR determined from the frequency data. It tells us that the odds of being in proficiency category 5 for a boy is .466 times the odds for a girl.

For many researchers, it is easier to interpret the OR than to interpret the logits, but the logits can also be interpreted directly. The effect for *gender* in the logistic regression model tells us how much the logit is expected to change when the value for *gender* changes by one unit, in this case from 0 (female) to 1 (male). Based on the Wald criteria, the effect of *gender* is statistically significant in the logit model: Wald's $\chi^2_1 = 24.690$, $p = .000$. This implies that the estimated slope for *gender* is −.765 and is statistically different from 0, and that the OR = $\exp(−.765) = .466$ is therefore statistically different from 1.0.

In this SPSS example, the deviance of the null model is found in the section for Block 1, "Iteration History," footnote c of Figure 3.1: $D_0 = −2LL_0 = 972.974$. The deviance of the fitted model containing only the variable *gender* is $D_m = −2LL_m = 947.825$. The difference between these two deviances is $G_m = 25.149$, $df = 1$, $p = .000$. For this example, with only one independent variable included in the model, the omnibus test is also the likelihood ratio test (an alternative to the Wald χ^2 test) for the effect of *gender*. The

20

Logistic Regression

Case Processing Summary

Unweighted Cases[a]		N	Percent
Selected Cases	Included in Analysis	702	100.0
	Missing Cases	0	.0
	Total	702	100.0
Unselected Cases		0	.0
Total		702	100.0

a. If weight is in effect, see classification table for the total number of cases.

Dependent Variable Encoding

Original Value	Internal Value
.00	0
1.00	1

Block 1: Method = Enter

Iteration History[a,b,c,d]

Iteration		−2 Log-likelihood	Coefficients Constant	gender
Step 1	1	947.829	.424	−.755
	2	947.825	.430	−.765
	3	947.825	.430	−.765

a. Method: Enter
b. Constant is included in the model.
c. Initial −2 Log-Likelihood: 972.974
d. Estimation terminated at iteration number 3 because parameter estimates changed by less than .001.

Omnibus Tests of Model Coefficients

		Chi-Square	df	Sig.
Step 1	Step	25.149	1	.000
	Block	25.149	1	.000
	Model	25.149	1	.000

Figure 3.1   Selected Output: SPSS Logistic Regression Example

Figure 3.1 (Continued)

Model Summary

Step	−2 Log-likelihood	Cox & Snell R Square	Nagelkerke R Square
1	947.825	.035	.047

Classification Table[a]

			Predicted		
			CUMSP2		Percentage
Observed			.00	1.00	Correct
Step 1	CUMSP2	.00	211	134	61.2
		1.00	151	206	57.7
	Overall Percentage				59.4

a. The cut value is .500.

Variables in the Equation

		B	S.E.	Wald	df	Sig.	Exp(B)	95.0% C.I. for EXP(B) Lower	Upper
Step 1[a]	gender	−.765	.154	24.690	1	.000	.466	.344	.629
	Constant	.430	.111	15.014	1	.000	1.537		

a. Variable(s) entered on step 1: gender.

omnibus test, found in "Omnibus Tests of Model Coefficients," means that we find a statistically significant decrease in the −2LL when *gender* is included in the model. This reduction represents a proportionate reduction in deviance that can be expressed through the likelihood ratio R^2_L: 1 − (D_m/D_0) = .0258. For this model, the inclusion of *gender* in the model reduces the deviance of the null model ($D_0 = -2LL_0$) by 2.58%.

Neither SPSS nor SAS reports R^2_L in their logistic regression procedures, but as shown above, it can be calculated easily from the available statistics provided in either package. Both statistical packages report two variations on the R^2 statistic for logit analysis: the Cox and Snell R^2, which SAS reports as the (generalized) R^2, and the Nagelkerke R^2, which SAS refers to as the "max-rescaled R²." The Nagelkerke R^2 rescales the Cox and Snell R^2 value to obtain a bound of 1.0. For these data, the "Model Summary" table of Figure 3.1 reports $R^2_{CS} = .035$ and $R^2_N = .047$. Although the omnibus test is statistically significant, none of the R^2 statistics is very large, suggesting that other explanatory variables in addition to *gender* may be helpful in understanding the likelihood of a child being in proficiency category 5. Menard (2000) discusses several attempts to generalize the familiar R^2 from ordinary linear regression, but he advocates R^2_L as the most useful of the available pseudo R^2's.

Attempting to reduce the fit assessment to a single value, as the collection of pseudo R^2's do, may have value in terms of comparing across competing (nested) models, but this provides only a "rough index of whether a model is adequate" (Long, 1997, p. 102). An investigation of model adequacy can be augmented by assessing how well the observed categorical outcomes are reproduced, based on whether or not an individual is predicted to fall into his or her original outcome of $Y = 0$ or $Y = 1$. This assessment of predictive efficiency supplements the information available from the tests for model fit and the reduction in deviance statistics. Some measures of fit or correspondence between observed and predicted outcomes are strongly influenced by data that are highly unbalanced in terms of distribution of frequency of the outcome, so an informed decision is best made by computing and comparing across several different measures rather than relying on one single measure.

To consider the ability of a model to correctly classify cases, classification is based on the probabilities estimated from the model, and the results are compared with the observed frequencies for each category. For any child, if the probability of "success" based on the logistic model is greater than .5, the predicted outcome would be 1; or else the predicted outcome would be 0 (Hosmer & Lemeshow, 2000; Long, 1997). SPSS produces a classification table directly, shown under Block 1: "Classification Table." The predicted probabilities can be requested in SAS (as well as in SPSS) to construct the classification table; review the syntax in Appendix A, sections A1 and A2, for how to save these predicted probabilities. Although many different kinds of classification statistics are available (Allison, 1999; Gibbons, 1993; Hosmer & Lemeshow, 2000; Huynh, 2002; Liebetrau, 1983; Long, 1997; Menard, 1995, 2000), several seem to be reported in the literature in preference to others and can be used with ordinal dependent variables. These include τ_p, which "adjusts the expected number of errors for the base rate of the classification" (Menard, 1995, p. 29), and the *adjusted count* R^2 or $R^2_{adjCount}$, which is similar to the Goodman-Kruskal λ in its asymmetric form (that is, when one variable is being predicted from a set of other variables); $R^2_{adjCount}$ adjusts the raw percentage correct measure for the likely probability of a case being assigned to the modal category of the observed dependent variable (DV) by chance (Liebetrau, 1983; Long, 1997). Unfortunately, there are often several different names for the same measures within the literature, and the reader of multiple articles or texts should pay close attention to the nomenclature that each author uses. For example, Menard (1995, 2000) refers to $R^2_{adjCount}$ as λ_p.

Hosmer and Lemeshow (2000) point out that model fit in terms of correspondence between observed and estimated probabilities is often more reliable and meaningful than an assessment of fit based on classification. They suggest that classification statistics be used as an adjunct to other measures, rather than as a sole indicator of quality of the model. As mentioned above, multiple criteria for investigating adequacy of fit of the models are demonstrated and reported in the examples covered here.

Neither SAS nor SPSS provides τ_p or λ_p ($R^2_{adjCount}$) directly, but they can be calculated once the classification table is obtained. To find τ_p, the expected number of errors must first be determined, and for 2 × 2 tables, this is

$$E(\text{errors}) = 2 \times \frac{f(Y=0) \times f(Y=1)}{n}.$$

The desired measure of association can then be calculated from

$$\tau_p = \frac{E(\text{errors}) \times O(\text{errors})}{E(\text{errors})}.$$

The observed errors are the off-diagonal elements of the classification table. A different expression for τ_p can be found in Menard (2000); it is also appropriate for ordinal response models:

$$\tau_p = 1 - \frac{\left(n - \sum_i f_{ii}\right)}{\sum_i \frac{f_i(n - f_i)}{n}},$$

where i represents the index for each category of the outcome variable, n = sample size, f_{ii} = sum of the correctly predicted categories (on the diagonal of the classification table), and f_i = the observed frequency for category i. For these data, $\tau_p = .1878$, indicating that after adjustment for the base rate, classification error is reduced by approximately 19% using the model with *gender* as the only predictor.

To find the R^2_{adjCount} or λ_p for the classification table, following Long (1997) and Menard (2000), the following calculation is used:

$$\lambda_p = 1 - \frac{n - \sum_i f_{ii}}{n - n_{\text{mode}}} = \frac{\sum_i f_{ii} - n_{\text{mode}}}{n - n_{\text{mode}}},$$

where n_{mode} is the frequency of observed responses in the modal category of the outcome (maximum row marginal). For these data, $\lambda_p = .1739$ with the observed categories treated as the dependent variable. For the model constructed in the above example, predicting proficiency category membership (0, 1 versus 5) based on *gender* reduces the prediction error by 17.4%, once the marginal distribution of the DV is taken into account.

SAS produces several ordinal measures of association within the LOGISTIC procedure that can supplement the pseudo R^2's and the statistics for predictive efficiency determined from the classification table, such as Somers' D, a rank order correlation statistic (Cliff, 1996a; Liebetrau, 1983). Most of the rank order statistics are based on the notion of concordant versus discordant pairs. The term "pair" refers to pairing of each case (individual) with every other case in the data set (not including itself). For a sample of size n, there are $n(n-1)/2$ possible pairings of individuals. Of interest are pairs of individuals that do not have the same observed response; we ignore pairings for which both cases are 0 or both cases are 1 on the outcome of interest. If the two cases have dissimilar responses, the pair is called concordant when the predicted probability (of being classified as "success" based on the model) for the case with the observed value of 1 is higher than the case with the observed value of 0; otherwise, the pair is termed discordant. A pair (with dissimilar response) is tied if it cannot be classified as either concordant or discordant (this would happen if the predicted probabilities were very close; SAS categorizes predicted probabilities into interval lengths of .002 (SAS, 1997). The effect is to count the number of times the direction of prediction is accurate for each pair of individuals with different outcomes. Somers' D is probably the most widely used of the available rank order correlation statistics: Somers' D = (nc − nd)/t; where nc = number of concordant pairs, nd = number of discordant pairs, and t = number of pairs with different responses. Using SAS, Somers' D for this example is .189, which represents the strength of the correspondence between observed outcomes and predicted probabilities.[8]

Comparing Results Across Statistical Programs

To facilitate use and interpretation of logistic analysis across different statistical packages, as well as to lead into our discussion of the treatment of ordinal outcomes, the previous model was also fit using SAS PROC LOGISTIC (both descending and ascending approaches) and SPSS PLUM (for ordinal outcomes). A summary of results is shown in Table 3.2 (syntax for these models appears in Appendix A, sections A1–A4). All models used the logit link function.

TABLE 3.2
Comparison of Results for SPSS, SAS, and SPSS PLUM for a
Dichotomous Outcome: Proficiency (0, 1 versus 5)[a] by Gender, $N = 702$

	SPSS Logistic and SAS (descending)	SAS (ascending)	SPSS PLUM
Probability estimated	$P(Y=1)$	$P(Y=0)$	$P(Y \leq 0)$
Intercept	.430	−.430	.335
gender = 1 (male)	−.765**	.765**	0
gender = 0 (female)			.765**
Model fit			
−2LL (intercept only)	972.94	972.974	972.974[b]
−2LL (model)	947.825	947.825	947.825
$\chi_1^2 (p)$	25.149 (< .0001)	25.149 (< .0001)	25.149 (< .0001)
Model predictions ($\hat{p}$)			
Male	.417	.583	.583
Female	.606	.394	.394

a. $Y = 0$ if response proficiency is 0 or 1; $Y = 1$ if response proficiency is 5.
b. Use "kernel" in the print command for SPSS PLUM to request the full value of the likelihoods.
**$p < .01$.

Reviewing the results in the first column of Table 3.2, note that SPSS LOGISTIC REGRESSION and SAS PROC LOGISTIC (descending) are fitting the same model based around estimating $P(Y = 1)$, which is the probability that a child has a response in proficiency category 5. The probability predictions for these two identical models can be found by first calculating the logit for boys and girls using the estimates provided, exponentiating these logits to determine the odds for each group, and then transforming these odds back into probability for the response identified as "success" ($p = $ [odds(success)/(1 + odds(success))]).

The results for the second model, shown in Column 3 of Table 3.2, using SAS with the ascending option, simply model the probability that a child has a response in proficiency category 0 or 1, rather than the probability that a child has a response in category 5. Notice that the signs on the intercept and the effect for *gender* are reversed from those in Column 2, yet they are of the same magnitude. Also note that the sum of the probability estimates for boys in Columns 2 and 3 is equal to 1.0, and similarly for girls. SAS with the descending option (Column 2) models the complement of the event from the default approach (ascending, in Column 3). Thus, the probabilities derived from the ascending approach are the complementary probabilities to those found when using SAS with the descending option.

The model parameter estimates using SPSS PLUM look very different from those obtained using the earlier approaches, but in fact the probability estimates are identical to those in Column 3 (and therefore, by the rule of complements, can be used to find the probability estimates in Column 2). SPSS PLUM is a program specifically designed for analyzing ordinal response variables, and the resulting parameter estimates will not exactly correspond to those found under SPSS Logistic Regression. In particular, the probability being estimated in SPSS PLUM is the probability of a response being *at or below* a particular outcome value, that is, the lower category codes; in contrast, SPSS LOGISTIC models the probability of the category with the higher outcome value. Additionally, whereas SAS handles both dichotomous and ordinal responses through its LOGISTIC procedure, the SPSS PLUM procedure uses a slightly different formulation of the generalized linear model that looks like: $\ln(Y'_j) = \theta_j - \beta_1 X_1$. In this expression, the subscript j refers to the response category, and X_1 refers to the single independent variable, *gender*. The estimate for the effect of *gender* is *subtracted* from the intercept. Another important distinction between PLUM results and those from logistic regression programs under SPSS or SAS is that PLUM internally sets up the coding for categorical predictors. In Column 4, the estimate provided for the *gender* effect corresponds to when *gender* = 0, that is, for females. The coding system used is clearly displayed on the printout (examples of PLUM and SAS printouts for ordinal models will be included in the next chapters). To find the estimated probability for a girl being (at most) in proficiency categories 0 or 1—that is, $P(Y \le 0)$—which is equivalent in this case to $P(Y = 0)$ because there are no responses less than 0, we use the estimates to find the predicted logit for girls (.335 − .765 = −.43), exponentiate the result to find the odds for girls of being at (or below) $Y = 0$ (exp(−.43) = .65), and then solve for the estimated probability (.65/(1 + .65) = .394). The same process is used to find the estimated probability for boys of being at (or below) categories 0 or 1, or $P(Y = 0)$.

SPSS PLUM provides R^2_L, referred to as *McFadden's pseudo R^2* (Long, 1997; Menard, 2000), in addition to R^2_{CS} and R^2_N. In order to obtain the necessary values for the $-2LL$ deviance statistics, the "*kernel*" option must be specified in the SPSS PLUM "*/print*" statement, as shown in syntax A4 in Appendix A.

The previous discussion and simple comparison of how SAS and SPSS treat binary outcomes illustrate that although model parameter estimates may vary on the surface, the resulting predicted probabilities computed from the model estimates, as well as model fit statistics, are consistent across packages and approaches. These simple examples also illustrate that it is important for an analyst to be aware of the outcome being predicted as well as how categorical independent variables are incorporated into the models, once a statistical package is selected. Distinctions across approaches and packages become even more critical as the number of categories for an ordinal response variable increases beyond the binary case.

4. THE CUMULATIVE (PROPORTIONAL) ODDS MODEL FOR ORDINAL OUTCOMES

Overview of the Cumulative Odds Model

With only two categories for an outcome variable, logistic regression is used to model the likelihood of one of the outcomes, usually termed the "success," as a function of a set of independent variables. The estimated probabilities for the response of interest, P(success), as well as for its complement, $1 - P$(success), can be determined using the prediction model for the logits, as shown in the example in Chapter 3. When the possible responses for an outcome variable consist of more than two categories and are ordinal in nature, the notion of "success" can be conceived of in many different ways. Regression models for ordinal response variables are designed for just this situation and are extensions of the logistic regression model for dichotomous data. The complexity in fitting ordinal regression models arises in part because there are so many different possibilities for how "success," and the consequent probability of "success," might be modeled.

For example, given a K-level ordinal response variable, such as proficiency in early literacy with $K = 6$ as in the ECLS-K study (Table 2.1), we could derive several different representations of "success" depending on how we view the data. In general, K-level ordinal data can be partitioned by $K - 1$ "success" cutpoints (Fox, 1997; McCullagh & Nelder, 1983). Success is, of course, a relative term; generally, it designates an event of interest. For example, "success" might be defined as having a child score in category 0 on the mastery test, that is, those children who were not able to recognize upper- and/or lowercase letters. Under this partitioning of the data, our interest would be in identifying factors associated with increased likelihood of being in this lowest category, rather than being beyond category 0, in categories 1 through 5. Perhaps there are harmful child, family, or school characteristics associated with increased probability of being in this lowest category. For these explanatory variables, we would calculate the odds of being at (or below) category 0.

We could next conceive of "success" as being at or below category 1; our interest in this partitioning of the data would be in identifying factors associated with greater likelihood of being in categories 0 or 1 relative to the likelihood of being beyond the lowest stages, in categories 2 through 5. We could continue to describe the data in this cumulative fashion, with the final conceptualization of "success" as being at or below the Kth category, which of course will always occur. Hence, the last split or partitioning of the data becomes unnecessary. Using this cumulative progression, we would have $K - 1$, or 5, distinct possible "success" characterizations of the data, given $K = 6$ ordinal response categories.

The analysis that mimics this method of dichotomizing the outcome, in which the successive dichotomizations form cumulative "splits" to the data, is referred to as proportional or cumulative odds (CO) (Agresti, 1996; Armstrong & Sloan, 1989; Long, 1997; McCullagh, 1980; McCullagh & Nelder, 1983). It is one way to conceptualize how the data might be sequentially partitioned into dichotomous groups, while still taking advantage of the order of the response categories. The ordinal nature of this approach is so appealing because of its similarity to logistic regression. If a single model could be used to estimate the odds of being *at or below* a given category across all cumulative splits, that model would offer far greater parsimony over the fitting of $K - 1$ different logistic regression models corresponding to the sequential partitioning of the data, as described above. The goal of the cumulative odds model is to simultaneously consider the effects of a set of independent variables across these possible consecutive cumulative splits to the data. There are other approaches, however, to defining "success." Each different method for performing ordinal regression characterizes the partitioning of the data in a very distinct way, and therefore they address very different research questions. The conceptualizations of how the data may be split to correspond to the cumulative odds (CO) model, as well as for the two other methods to fitting ordinal regression models that I will discuss in this book, the continuation ratio (CR) model and the adjacent categories (AC) model, are provided in the indicated columns of

29

Table 4.1. The latter two approaches will be discussed fully in later chapters. This chapter focuses on the CO model.

A simplifying assumption is made of the data when applying ordinal regression models, and that is the assumption of proportional, or parallel, odds. This assumption implies that the explanatory variables have the same effect on the odds, regardless of the different consecutive splits to the data, for each category of model (CO, CR, AC), as shown in Table 4.1. For example, if the set of separate binary logistic regressions corresponding to the CO model described above were fit to the data, the assumption of parallelism implies that a common odds ratio (or effect) for a variable would be observed across all the regressions; the effect of an IV on the odds is assumed to be invariant across the corresponding splits (Agresti, 1989; Brant, 1990; Menard, 1995; Peterson & Harrell, 1990). Thus, one model would be sufficient to describe the relationship between the ordinal response variable and a set of predictors.

Both SAS and SPSS provide a score test for the proportional odds assumption within their ordinal regression procedures, but this omnibus test for proportionality is not a powerful test and is anticonservative (Peterson & Harrell, 1990); the test nearly always results in very small p values, particularly when the number of explanatory variables is large (Brant, 1990), the sample size is large (Allison, 1999; Clogg & Shihadeh, 1994), or continuous explanatory variables are included in the model (Allison, 1999). Therefore, conclusions about rejecting the null hypothesis of proportionality of the odds based solely on the score test should be made cautiously. Rejection of the assumption of parallelism (proportional odds) for the particular ordinal model being investigated implies that at least one of the explanatory variables may be having a differential effect across the outcome levels, that is, that there is an interaction between one or more of the independent variables and the derived splits to the data (Armstrong & Sloan, 1989; Peterson & Harrell, 1990). The key is to be able to identify which variable(s) may be contributing to rejection of this overall test.

A reasonable strategy for investigating whether the effects of the independent variables are relatively stable or not across the cumulative logits is through comparison of variable effects across the separate logistic regression models that correspond to the ordinal model being considered, as in Table 4.1. Although the simplifying assumption of proportionality may be useful in terms of fitting an overall model to the data, it has been recommended that researchers examine the underlying binary models in order to supplement decisions about the aptness of an ordinal approach (Brant, 1990; Clogg & Shihadeh, 1994; Long, 1997; O'Connell, 2000). Informal comparison of the slopes across the corresponding separate logistic fits for a model can provide supportive information regarding the plausibility of parallelism for the data. Later in this chapter, an approach that relaxes the

30

TABLE 4.1

Category Comparisons Associated With
Three Different Ordinal Regression Model Approaches,
Based on a 6-Level Ordinal Outcome (j = 0, 1, 2, 3, 4, 5)

Cumulative Odds (ascending) $P(Y \leq j)$	Cumulative Odds (descending) $P(Y \geq j)$	Continuation Ratio $P(Y > j \vert Y \geq j)$	Adjacent Categories $P(Y = j + 1 \vert Y = j$ or $Y = j + 1)$
Category 0 versus all above	Category 5 versus all below	Categories 1 through 5 versus category 0	Category 1 versus category 0
Categories 0 and 1 combined versus all above	Categories 5 and 4 versus all below	Categories 2 through 5 versus category 1	Category 2 versus category 1
Categories 0, 1, and 2 combined versus all above	Categories 5, 4, and 3 versus all below	Categories 3 through 5 versus category 2	Category 3 versus category 2
Categories 0, 1, 2, and 3 combined versus all above	Categories 5, 4, 3, and 2 versus all below	Categories 4 and 5 versus category 3	Category 4 versus category 3
Categories 0, 1, 2, 3 and 4 combined versus category 5	Categories 5, 4, 3, 2, and 1 versus category 0	Category 5 versus category 4	Category 5 versus category 4

proportional odds assumption for some explanatory variables, the *partial proportional odds* (PPO) model (Ananth & Kleinbaum, 1997; Koch, Amara, & Singer, 1985; Peterson & Harrell, 1990), is presented.

EXAMPLE 4.1: Cumulative Odds Model With a Single Explanatory Variable

To illustrate the use of the cumulative odds model, I begin by fitting a simple model with just one categorical explanatory variable: *gender*. Table 4.2 provides the frequency of each of the five early-reading proficiency categories for boys and girls. The data are unbalanced across proficiency categories, with most children, regardless of *gender*, falling into proficiency category 3. This characteristic of the data can be an important consideration when deciding among models (CO, CR, AC, or others) that might best represent the data; however, for pedagogical purposes we will ignore this characteristic of the data for now, then reexamine its impact after the different ordinal models have been presented.

The cumulative odds model is used to predict the odds of being *at or below* a particular category. Because there are *K* possible ordinal outcomes, the model actually makes *K* − 1 predictions, each corresponding to the accumulation of probability across successive categories. If we let $\pi(Y \leq j|x_1, x_2, \ldots x_p) = \pi_j(\underline{x})$ represent the probability that a response falls in a category less than or equal to the *j*th category (*j* = 1, 2, ... *K* − 1), then we have a collection of cumulative probabilities for each case. The final category will always have a cumulative probability of 1.0. (Note that in the ECLS-K data, I use category 0 to refer to the first category, and the *K* = 6th category is proficiency category 5.) With an extension from the general logistic regression model, the predictions are logits for the *cumulative* probabilities, which are referred to as *cumulative logits*:

$$\ln(Y'_j) = \ln\left(\frac{\pi_j(\underline{x})}{1 - \pi_j(\underline{x})} \right) = \alpha_j + (\beta_1 X_1 + \beta_2 X_2 + \ldots \beta_p X_p).$$

The cumulative logits associated with being at or below a particular category *j* can be exponentiated to arrive at the estimated cumulative odds and then used to find the estimated cumulative probabilities associated with being at or below category *j*.

Table 4.2 also contains the cross-tabulation of the ECLS-K data in terms of actual probabilities (*p*), cumulative probabilities (*cp*), and cumulative odds (*co*) for boys and girls of being in category *j* or below. The **bold** row contains the associated odds ratios (boys:girls) for these data. The last two rows of the table provide the category totals and the cumulative proportion ($P(Y_i \leq$ category *j*)) regardless of *gender*. From the table, we see that the odds of being at or below any specific category increases as the response value increases, for both boys and girls. This makes intuitive sense, as within the sample there are fewer children who are in the highest categories; children are more likely to be at or below a given category than beyond that category. In general, the odds for boys are always greater than the odds for girls, as proportionately fewer boys than girls in the sample reached the higher proficiency categories when tested at the beginning of first grade. The odds ratios make this pattern clear. The odds that boys are *at or below* a specific category are about 1.72 (on average) times the odds for girls of being *at or below* that category. The likelihood is that girls tend to exceed boys on this ordinal measure of proficiency at the beginning of first grade.

Similar to the example in Chapter 3, I am going to present results for this simple one-variable CO model using three different approaches: SAS PROC LOGISTIC, SAS PROC LOGISTIC with a "descending" option, and SPSS PLUM (syntax for all models is provided in the

TABLE 4.2

Observed Data Cross-Classification of Gender by Five Proficiency
Categories: Frequency (f), Proportion (p), Cumulative Proportion (cp),
Cumulative Odds[a] (co), and Odds Ratios (OR)

Category	0	1	2	3	4	5	Totals (f)
Males							
f	48	163	320	735	256	151	1673
p	.0278	.0974	.1913	.4393	.1530	.0903	1.000
cp	.0278	.1261	.3174	.7567	.9097	1.000	—
co	.0295	.1443	.4650	3.110	10.074	—	—
Females							
f	19	115	274	747	331	206	1692
p	.0112	.0680	.1619	.4415	.1956	.1217	1.000
cp	.0112	.0792	.2411	.6826	.8782	.9999	—
co	.0113	.0860	.3177	2.1506	7.210	—	—
OR	**2.6106**	**1.6779**	**1.4636**	**1.446**	**1.3972**	—	—
Totals (f)	67	278	594	1482	587	357	3,365
cp_{total}	.0199	.1025	.2790	.7195	.8939	1.000	—

a. Cumulative odds = Odds($Y_i \leq$ category j).

Appendix, section B). Figure 4.1 displays the SAS output (with the default
"ascending" approach) for this simple one-variable cumulative odds model.
The appropriate link function for the cumulative odds model is the logit
link. To run this model, I used the SAS syntax in section B1 of the appendix. The syntax for the other two approaches to the CO model is in sections B2 and B3. Although these approaches are essentially identical in
terms of prediction when the CO model is desired, such is not necessarily
the case with the CR and AC ordinal regression models. It is important to
be clear on the similarities and differences among programs and
approaches, beginning with the simplest case of the CO model.

Using SAS (ascending), the odds are accumulated over the lower-ordered
categories. That is, the associated predicted cumulative probabilities correspond to the pattern shown in the first column of Table 4.1. SAS is estimating the $P(Y \leq$ category $j)$, which for these data are $P(Y \leq 0)$, $P(Y \leq 1)$,
$P(Y \leq 2)$, $P(Y \leq 3)$, $P(Y \leq 4)$, and of course $P(Y \leq 5) = 1.0$ for the final category (which typically is not included on printouts of these analyses). A
reliable CO model would reproduce the cumulative odds and cumulative
probabilities found from the data in Table 4.2.

In the models presented here, *gender* is coded as 0 for girls and 1 for
boys. Reviewing the output provided in Figure 4.1, we see that the proportional odds assumption is upheld for these data ("Score Test for the

```
The LOGISTIC Procedure

                    Model Information

      Data Set                     WORK.GONOMISS
      Response Variable            PROFREAD
      Number of Response Levels    6
      Number of Observations       3365
      Model                        cumulative logit
      Optimization Technique       Fisher's scoring

                  Response Profile

      Ordered                         Total
      Value         PROFREAD        Frequency
        1            0.00              67
        2            1.00             278
        3            2.00             594
        4            3.00            1482
        5            4.00             587
        6            5.00             357

        Probabilities modeled are cumulated
          over the lower Ordered Values.

            Model Convergence Status

     Convergence criterion (GCONV=1E-8) satisfied.

     Score Test for the Proportional Odds Assumption

         Chi-Square       DF       Pr > ChiSq
          5.3956           4         0.2491

                Model Fit Statistics

                      Intercept        Intercept
      Criterion         OnlY         and Covariates
      AIC             10063.980        10028.591
      SC              10094.586        10065.319
      -2 Log L        10053.980        10016.591


              The LOGISTIC Procedure

    R-Square    0.0110    Max-rescaled R-Square    0.0116

        Testing Global Null Hypothesis: BETA=0

    Test                 Chi-Square      DF      Pr > ChiSq

    Likelihood Ratio      37.3884        1       <.0001
    Score                 37.2553        1       <.0001
    Wald                  37.2060        1       <.0001
```

Figure 4.1   SAS Cumulative Odds Model Example: *Gender*

Figure 4.1 (Continued)

```
         Analysis of Maximum Likelihood Estimates

                            Standard      Wald        Pr >
Parameter        DF  Estimate   Error   Chi-Square    ChiSq

Intercept 0.00    1   -4.1049   0.1284   1022.2632    <.0001
Intercept 1.00    1   -2.3739   0.0667   1266.5201    <.0001
Intercept 2.00    1   -1.1474   0.0510    505.4293    <.0001
Intercept 3.00    1    0.7590   0.0485    245.3247    <.0001
Intercept 4.00    1    1.9545   0.0627    971.9783    <.0001
GENDER            1    0.3859   0.0633     37.2060    <.0001


                 Odds Ratio Estimates

                   Point      95% Wald

     Effect        Estimate        Confidence       Limits
     GENDER         1.471            1.299           1.665


         Association of Predicted Probabilities
                and Observed Responses

    Percent Concordant       29.0      Somers' D    0.079
    Percent Discordant       21.1      Gamma        0.159
    Percent Tied             49.9      Tau-a        0.058
    Pairs                 4110137      c            0.540
```

Proportional Odds Assumption"), $\chi^2_4 = 5.3956$, $p = .2491$. We can conclude that the effect of *gender* is not statistically different across the five cumulative splits for the data; this implies that if five separate binary logistic models were fit corresponding to the pattern in Table 4.1, the slopes (and odds ratios) for *gender* in each of these models would be similar. Thus, the *gender* ORs could be estimated simultaneously using only one model. Because *gender* is the only variable included here, this result also tells us that the five ORs in Table 4.2 are not statistically different, and that one common OR could be used to summarize the effect of *gender* on proficiency.

The pseudo R^2 statistics are found in the "Model Fit Statistics" section of the printout (Figure 4.1), in the line under "The LOGISTIC Procedure," with the Cox and Snell $R^2_{CS} = .0110$ and the Nagelkerke (which SAS refers to as Max-rescaled R-Square) $R^2_N = .0116$. The likelihood ratio $R^2_L = .0037$ can be calculated using the –2loglikelihood statistics for the intercepts-only model and the intercepts plus covariates model information contained in the "Model Fit Statistics" summary table. Collectively, these R^2 statistics suggest that the relationship between the response and predictor variables is a weak one. However, the tests for overall model fit ("Testing Global Null Hypothesis"), which assess whether the fitted model improves predictions over those presented by the null (intercepts-only) model, are all statistically significant, so we reject the null model in favor of the model that includes *gender* as a predictor. Despite the low pseudo R^2 values, the likelihood ratio test suggests that the pattern of cumulative proportions for boys and girls as predicted from the model (see Table 4.3; entries explained later) provides a better match to the actual cumulative proportions for boys and girls (shown in Table 4.2) than what would be expected disregarding *gender* (last row of Table 4.2). This simple CO model makes clear how these proportions are different for boys versus girls.

The next section of the printout (Figure 4.1) contains "Analysis of Maximum Likelihood Estimates," a table with five intercepts, referred to as threshold parameters: one for each of the $K - 1$ cutpoints. It is useful to think of these thresholds as marking the point (in terms of a logit) at which children might be predicted into the higher categories, but they are not usually interpreted individually, similar to how the intercept functions in an ordinary multiple regression model. However, with dummy coding for *gender* (*gender* = 0 for girls), these threshold estimates represent the predicted logits corresponding to $Y \leq$ category j for girls. The effect of *gender* on the logit is .3859, with an associated odds ratio of 1.471 (exp(.3859) = 1.471). The model informs us that the odds for boys of being at or below category j are about 1.471 times the odds for girls, regardless of which cumulative split we are considering. This result can be compared with the pattern we saw using the observed data in Table 4.2, where the average OR across

TABLE 4.3
Predicted Cumulative Logits, Estimated Odds of
Being at or Below Category j for Boys and Girls,
Estimated Cumulative Probabilities (*cp*), and Estimated
Odds Ratios From the CO Model (SAS With Ascending Option)

Comparison	$(Y \leq 0)$	$(Y \leq 1)$	$(Y \leq 2)$	$(Y \leq 3)$	$(Y \leq 4)$
Boys					
Cumulative logit	−3.719	−1.988	−.7615	1.1449	2.3404
Cumulative odds	.02427	.13696	.4670	3.1421	10.385
$\hat{cp}_b$	.0237	.1205	.3183	.7586	.9122
Girls					
Cumulative logit	−4.1049	−2.3739	−1.1474	.7590	1.9545
Cumulative odds	.0165	.0931	.3175	2.1363	7.0604
$\hat{cp}_g$	.0162	.0852	.2410	.6811	.8760
OR	**1.4711**	**1.4711**	**1.4709**	**1.4708**	**1.4709**

categories was 1.72. According to the model, boys are less likely to be *beyond* a particular category relative to girls, which is consistent with the actual data. Recall that this model assumes that the effect of *gender* is constant across the separate cumulative splits. Because we did not reject the assumption of proportional odds when *gender* was included as a predictor, the CO model suggests that the separate ORs for the cumulative splits (Table 4.2) are not statistically different from the OR of 1.471 found for the CO model.

Turning to a direct interpretation of the parameter estimates for the model, the intercepts and the effect of *gender* can be used to estimate the cumulative odds, that is, the odds of being at or below a given category for boys and for girls. These also can be used to estimate the ORs at each split, although we already know from our analysis that this is set at 1.471. The cumulative odds estimated for boys and girls can be compared back to those derived from the original data (Table 4.2). Predictions for girls, when *gender* = 0, correspond to the intercepts for each cumulative category, which when exponentiated provide the odds for girls of having a response at or below category *j*. Predictions for boys are found by substituting the value of *gender* = 1 into the cumulative odds model for each respective equation and exponentiating to find the odds: $\ln(Y'_j) = \alpha_j + .3859(gender)$. For example, for the logit representing $Y \leq 0$, the predicted logit for girls is –4.1049; for boys, the predicted logit is –3.719. Table 4.3 provides these *estimated cumulative logits* based on the model as well as the *estimated cumulative odds* (*co*) for boys and girls (exp(cum. logit)). From these predicted cumulative odds, odds ratios comparing boys to girls can be found easily for each category, and these are shown in the last row of Table 4.3 (e.g., co_{boys}/co_{girls}). Within rounding error, the ORs are all approximately 1.47. The estimated cumulative odds are transformed into the estimated cumulative probabilities (*cp*) using $cp = (co/[1 + co])$, which yields $P(Y \leq$ category *j*). The results are shown in Table 4.3 and can be compared with the observed cumulative probabilities presented in Table 4.2. Overall, the estimates seem to match the data well; recall that the likelihood ratio test was statistically significant for this model.

The model predictions make it clear what the assumption of proportional odds means for these data. The OR is fixed, and therefore remains constant across all cumulative categories, implying that overall, the odds for boys of being at or below any category *j* are about 1.47 times the odds for girls of being at or below category *j*. For this sample, boys are more likely than girls to be *at or below* any given category; girls are more likely than boys to be in *higher* categories. *Gender* (male = 1) has a positive effect (*b* = .3859) on the cumulative logit, corresponding to larger odds of being *at or below* category *j* for boys relative to girls. This last interpretation is consistent with the transformed outcome being modeled in this approach (response *at or below* category *j*), and hence the interpretation of the direction of the logit and the effects of explanatory variables hinge on how the outcome is characterized. Differences between estimated and actual cumulative probabilities are due to the fact that the CO model is imposing a very specific structure on the data. This structure is evidenced through the behavior of the ORs, and thus it affects the cumulative proportions estimated from the model as well. The estimates for the cumulative probabilities are derived under the assumption of proportional odds. Although we saw earlier that this assumption is valid for our data across *gender*, it is important to recognize that the model estimates and the predicted probabilities are driven by this assumption. In situations where the assumption does not hold or seems empirically or theoretically implausible, these predicted probabilities could be grossly inaccurate. Unfortunately, when models become more complex, such as those that include additional explanatory variables, either categorical or continuous, it can become quite challenging to have confidence in the assumption of proportional odds. I will return to this topic toward the end of this chapter.

Somers' D for this analysis was .079 (see last section of Figure 4.1), which is quite low. With only one predictor, we are getting very weak concordance for the ordinal direction of predicted probabilities among pairs of children. To construct the classification table for the measures of predictive efficiency, τ_p and λ_p, we can use the collection of cumulative predicted probabilities for each child to assess where individual probability of category membership is at its maximum. With the "*predprobs = cumulative*" option specified in the output subcommand, SAS creates a data file containing the cumulative probabilities for the *i*th child at each level, $cp0_i = P$(at or below level 0), $cp1_i = P$(at or below level 1), and so on. Thus, each child has K new observations in the data set, with $cp5_i = P$(at or below level 5) = 1.0 for all children. Category probabilities can be found by using the relationship $P(Y = \text{category } j) = P(Y \leq \text{category } j) - P(Y \leq \text{category } [j-1])$. That is, $P_i(Y = 0) = cp0_i$; $P_i(Y = 1) = cp1_i - cp0_i$; $P_i(Y = 2) = cp2_i - cp1_i$; and so on. The maximum category probability for an individual child corresponds to his or her best prediction for proficiency level. In the *gender*-only, ascending model, all children are predicted into category 3, which is not surprising given that the model has weak fit and category 3 represents 44% of the children in this sample. Following the methods outlined in Chapter 3, the classification estimates can be tabled to the observed proficiency categories to calculate measures of predictive efficiency. For this analysis, τ_p and λ_p are .23 and 0, respectively. These results underscore the need to consider several different measures of association in conjunction with the likelihood ratio tests when assessing the reasonableness of a model.

38

Table 4.4 provides a comparison of the results for the SAS model just described, based on the "ascending" default option in the ordering of the ordinal dependent variable, with the results from SAS "descending," SPSS PLUM, and a multiple regression model with *gender* as the only predictor. Although the CO models are essentially the same and provide the same *interpretation* of the effect of *gender*, some important similarities and differences in the *presentation* of the results for these models should be pointed out.

First, similar to the results using the ascending and descending options in SAS PROC LOGISTIC with a dichotomous outcome, the estimates for the threshold (intercept) parameters are reversed in sign but not in magnitude; they also appear in reverse order on the printout. This is simply due to the fact that the descending and ascending options predict complementary events. With the descending option in place, the model is estimating the (reversed) cumulative odds, that is, $P(Y \geq 5)$, $P(Y \geq 4)$, $P(Y \geq 3)$, $P(Y \geq 2)$, and $P(Y \geq 1)$, and of course $P(Y \geq 0)$ will always equal 1.0.

TABLE 4.4

Results for Cumulative Odds Model Using
SAS (Ascending), SAS (Descending), SPSS PLUM, and
Multiple Linear Regression on an Ordinal Response Scale:
Proficiency ($j = 0$, 1, 2, 3, 4, 5) by Gender, $N = 3,365$

	SAS (ascending)	SAS (descending)	SPSS PLUM	SPSS REGRESSION
Model estimates	$P(Y \leq \text{cat. } j)$	$P(Y \geq \text{cat. } j)$	$P(Y \leq \text{cat. } j)$	$E(Y|X)$
Intercept α				3.108
Thresholds	$\alpha_0 = -4.105$	$\alpha_5 = -1.955$	$\theta_0 = -3.719$	
	$\alpha_1 = -2.374$	$\alpha_4 = -0.759$	$\theta_1 = -1.988$	
	$\alpha_2 = -1.147$	$\alpha_3 = 1.147$	$\theta_2 = -.762$	
	$\alpha_3 = 0.759$	$\alpha_2 = -2.374$	$\theta_3 = 1.145$	
	$\alpha_4 = 1.955$	$\alpha_1 = 4.105$	$\theta_4 = 2.340$	
gender = 1 (male)	.386**	-.386**	0	-.246**
gender = 0 (female)			.386**	
R^2	.004[a]	.004[a]	.004[a]	.012
Score test[b]	$\chi^2_4 = 5.3956$	$\chi^2_4 = 5.3956$	$\chi^2_4 = 5.590$	
	$(p = .2491)$	$(p = .2491)$	$(p = .232)$	
Model fit[c]	$\chi^2_1 = 37.388$	$\chi^2_1 = 37.388$	$\chi^2_1 = 37.388$	$F_{1, 3363} =$
	$(p < .001)$	$(p < .001)$	$(p < .001)$	40.151
				$(p < .001)$

a. R^2_L = likelihood ratio R^2.
b. For the proportional odds assumption.
c. Likelihood ratio test for ordinal models; F test for ordinary least squares (OLS) regression.
**$p < .01$.

Second, the score test for the proportional odds assumption indicates that the assumption of proportionality is upheld across the analyses, $\chi^2_4 = 5.3956$, $p > .05$, as would be expected, although SPSS refers to this as the "Test of Parallel Lines."[9] For all three models, the omnibus likelihood ratio tests indicate that the ordinal gender model fits better than the null, $\chi^2_1 = 37.388$, $p < .001$.

Third, predictions of the cumulative odds and cumulative proportions using SAS ascending and SPSS PLUM are exactly the same; and the predictions for the cumulative odds for SAS descending yield the complements of these probabilities. Recall that for SPSS PLUM, the model predictions are found by subtracting the effect of *gender* from the threshold estimates. SPSS PLUM also uses an internal coding system for the categorical predictors. For example, to estimate the cumulative probability for a girl having a proficiency response less than or equal to 2 using the PLUM model, we would (a) find $\ln(\text{odds}(Y \leq 2)) = \theta_2 - \beta_{(gender = 0)} = -.762 - (.386) = -1.148$; (b) exponentiate to find the odds, $\exp(-1.148) = .3173$; and (c) use these odds to find the cumulative probability for a girl, $P(Y \leq 2) = .3173/(1 + .3173) = .2409$, consistent with the SAS ascending results used for Table 4.3. To clarify the approach of SAS with the descending option, consider the complement of $Y \leq 2_{girls}$, that is, $Y \geq 3_{girls}$. Using the parameter estimates for the descending model in Table 4.4, we have cumulative $\log_{girls, Y \geq 3} = \alpha_3 + (-.386) \times gender = +1.147$ (because $gender = 0$ for girls). Then the cumulative $\text{odds}_{girls, Y \geq 3} = \exp(1.147) = 3.149$. The estimated probability is $P(Y \geq 3)_{girls} = 3.149/(1 + 3.149) = .759$. This is the complementary probability to $P(Y \leq 2)$ using either SAS ascending or SPSS PLUM; from Table 4.3, $1 - .2410 = .759$.

Fourth, as mentioned previously, all these programs can be asked to save estimated probabilities, which then can be compared easily (at least for models with a small number of predictors) with those for the original data. When running a CO model, SAS will calculate and save the *cumulative* probabilities, according to how you requested them (ascending or descending). SPSS PLUM, however, does not make the cumulative probabilities available directly, but instead calculates and saves the individual's category membership probabilities. As shown just above, the cumulative probabilities can be determined readily from the parameter estimate information provided for any of the three models.

Interpretations across the three models are identical, although the actual values of the thresholds and slopes are not similar between SPSS PLUM and SAS (ascending or descending). This is simply due to how the two packages parameterize the model being fit. Differences between the SAS ascending and descending approaches are seen readily in the reversal of signs and subscripts marking the thresholds. The cumulative odds for the *descending* approach are the odds of being *at or beyond* a particular proficiency level; the cumulative odds for the *ascending* approach and for PLUM are the odds of being *at or below* a particular proficiency level. The thresholds appear in reverse order on the output between the two SAS approaches, but once the predicted logits are transformed to cumulative probabilities, the results are essentially equivalent. The effect of *gender* is reversed in sign for the two SAS models, and in PLUM the *gender* effect corresponds to the case *gender* = 0, but the interested reader is urged to use these simple models to verify equivalence in predicted probabilities once the characterization of the model and the cumulative probabilities being derived are accounted for. An example of the treatment of *gender* across the three models is provided in the paragraphs to follow.

In SPSS PLUM, the threshold estimates are for the case when *gender* = 1 (males), whereas in SAS, the threshold estimates are for the case when *gender* = 0 (females). Regardless of the analysis used, the effect of *gender* is constant across all cumulative splits, $b = \pm.386$. For example, using SAS (ascending), the logit prediction for boys being in proficiency level 2 or lower is $\alpha_2 + b_{\text{gender(boys)}} = -1.147 + .386 = -.761$. This is equivalent to the prediction for boys following the SPSS PLUM analysis: $\theta_2 - b_{\text{gender(boys)}} = -.762 - 0 = -.762$. Exponentiating to find the cumulative odds and transforming the results to find predicted probability for boys of being at or below proficiency level 2, we have $P(Y \leq 2) = .318$ (see Table 4.3). The odds ratios for boys:girls across all cumulative splits are assumed constant based on the proportional odds model and are equivalent for SAS (ascending) and SPSS PLUM: $\exp(.386) = 1.47$; this indicates that the odds for boys of being at or below any category j are 1.47 times the odds for girls of being at or below any category j.

Using the SAS (descending) approach, we can say that the odds for boys being in category j *or beyond* relative to girls are constant across all cumulative splits: $\exp(-.386) = .680$, which implies that boys are less likely than girls to be *at or beyond* a given proficiency level. Interpreted slightly differently, this result shows that the odds for boys are .68 times the odds for girls of being *at or beyond* any category j. Girls are more likely to be in higher proficiency categories. Note that the odds ratios for either approach (ascending or descending) are inverses of each other: $1/.68 = 1.47$. Note also that the probability predictions for boys being at or below category j, for example, can be determined from the SAS (descending) model as well, because $P(Y \leq j) = 1 - P(Y \geq j + 1)$. As another example of this process, to find $P(Y \leq 2)$ for boys, we can use the descending model to find the cumulative logit for $Y \geq 3$ for boys, $\alpha_3 + b_{\text{gender(boys)}} = 1.147 + (-.386) = .761$; exponentiating and solving for cumulative probability, we find $P(Y \geq 3) = .682$; finally, $1 - .682 = P(Y \leq 2) = .318$, consistent with results shown in Table 4.3.

When results of these models are compared to the multiple regression (MR) analysis, we see a similar pattern in terms of boys being below girls in proficiency. The dependent variable of proficiency in this MR analysis is coded to be increasing in value from 0 to 5. The slope for the *gender* variable (boys = 1) is negative, –.246. On average, girls are predicted to be at a proficiency level of 3.109, whereas boys are predicted to be at a lower proficiency level of (3.109 – .246) = 2.863. Although globally there are similarities between the ordinal models and the MR model in terms of direction of the effect of *gender*, the predicted outcomes from the MR model are not consistent with the data we are analyzing. A mean proficiency score is not the value we wish to predict when our response values are strictly ordinal; furthermore, the MR model does not allow us to make classification statements where we might compare across the different proficiency levels.

EXAMPLE 4.2: Full-Model Analysis of Cumulative Odds

The analyses thus far indicate that the one-variable model could be improved upon. The predicted probabilities for the *gender*-only model under the proportional odds assumption are very similar to the actual cumulative proportions, and the likelihood ratio test results indicate that the cumulative probabilities when *gender* is included in the model are more consistent with the actual data than the null model (without *gender*). The R^2 statistics were very small, as were Somers' D and the measures of predictive efficiency. We now turn to the derivation of a more complex cumulative odds model to determine the relationship between additional explanatory variables and the cumulative probabilities across the six proficiency levels. Table 4.5 provides a summary of results for the fitting of the CO model with eight explanatory variables from Table 2.2 (recall that *public* is a school-level variable and will not be used in these single-level models). The results in Table 4.5 were obtained using SAS with the descending option; the probabilities being modeled are $P(Y \geq$ category $j)$. This approach was taken to facilitate later comparison with the CR and AC ordinal models. The syntax for the full CO model is contained in Appendix B, section B4.

The proportional odds assumption for this model is not upheld, as can be seen in the row of Table 4.5 labeled "score test." This suggests that the pattern of effects for one or more of the independent variables is likely to be different across separate binary models fit according to the pattern indicated earlier for the CO model in Table 4.1. Unfortunately, with continuous predictors and large sample sizes, the score test will nearly always indicate rejection of the assumption of proportional odds, and therefore should be interpreted cautiously (Allison, 1999; Greenland, 1994; Peterson & Harrell,

TABLE 4.5

Full-Model Analysis of Cumulative
Odds (CO), SAS (Descending) ($Y \geq$ cat. j), $N = 3,365$

Variable	b (se(b))	OR
α_5	−6.01 (.54)	
α_4	−4.73 (.53)	
α_3	−2.62 (.53)	
α_2	−1.30 (.53)	
α_1	.50 (.54)	
gender	−.50 (.06)**	.607
famrisk	−.26 (.08)**	.771
center	.09 (.08)	1.089
noreadbo	−.32 (.09)**	.729
minority	−.15 (.07)*	.862
halfdayK	−.17 (.07)*	.847
wksesl	.71 (.05)**	2.042
p1ageent	.06 (.01)**	1.063
R^2_L	.05	
Cox & Snell R^2	.14	
Nagelkerke R^2	.15	
Somers' D	.33	
τ_p	.21	
λ_p	.00	
Model fit[a]	$\chi^2_8 = 524.17$ ($p < .0001$)	
Score test[c]	$\chi^2_{32} = 75.47$ ($p < .0001$)	

a. Likelihood ratio test.
b. For the proportional odds assumption.
*$p < .05$; **$p < .01$.

1990). We will return to an examination of this assumption later; for now, let us interpret what the model estimates and fit statistics mean for this analysis.

The model fit chi-square indicates that this full model is performing better than the null model (no independent variables) at predicting cumulative probability for proficiency. We see some improvement in the likelihood ratio and pseudo R^2 statistics, but not much more than what was obtained using the *gender*-only model. Somers' D is .333, which is markedly better than what was obtained through the *gender*-only model.

Recall that proficiency was measured through six categories with outcomes as 0, 1, 2, 3, 4, or 5. With the descending option, the threshold estimates in Table 4.5 correspond to predictions of the cumulative logits for students who have a score of 0 on the complete set of independent variables; α_5 corresponds to the cumulative logit for $Y \geq 5$, α_4 corresponds to the cumulative logit for $Y \geq 4$, and so on, until α_1 corresponds to the cumulative logit for $Y \geq 1$. Because all students will have $Y \geq 0$, this first threshold is not included in the descending cumulative logit model (note that the same is true for $Y \leq 5$ for the ascending cumulative logit model). The effects of the independent variables within the full CO model shed some important light on how variables contribute to the probability of being at or beyond a particular category. Consistent with the earlier *gender*-only model, boys are less likely than girls to be beyond a particular category (OR = .607). The presence of any family risk factor (*famrisk*, OR = .771), having parents who do not read to their children (*noreadbo*, OR = .729), being in a minority category (*minority*, OR = .862), and attending half-day kindergarten rather than full-day kindergarten (*haldayK*, OR = .847) all have negative coefficients in the model and corresponding ORs that are significantly less than 1.0. These characteristics are associated with a child being in lower proficiency categories rather than in higher categories. On the other hand, age at kindergarten entry (*p1ageent*, OR = 1.063) and family SES (*wksesl*, OR = 2.042) are positively associated with higher proficiency categories. The slopes for both variables are positive and significantly different from zero in the multivariable model. Attending center-based day care prior to kindergarten (*center*) is not associated with proficiency in this model; the slope is small, and the OR is close to 1.0. These findings are consistent with the literature on factors affecting early literacy, and as such the full model provides a reasonable perspective of the way in which these selected variables affect proficiency in this domain.

In terms of predictive efficiency, neither τ_p or λ_p offers better category predictions relative to the *gender*-only model, which classified *all* children into category 3. For the full-model CO analysis, the cumulative probabilities can be used to determine individual category probabilities as described in the *gender*-only analysis, with the maximum category probability corresponding to the best proficiency level prediction for each child. Table 4.6 provides the results of the classification scheme based on the full CO model. Most of the children are still classified into proficiency level 3, and we can determine from the classification table (using the formulas presented in Chapter 3) that $\tau_p = .23$ and $\lambda_p = 0$, indicating no overall improvement in predictions from the *gender*-only analysis. This would be discouraging if category prediction was the sole goal of the model. However, as mentioned in the binary logistic regression example, these measures tell us very little as to *how* the explanatory variables are affecting estimates of cumulative probability across the proficiency levels. Hosmer and Lemeshow (2000) remark that classification is very sensitive to group size and "always favors classification into the larger group, a fact that is independent of the fit of the model" (p. 157). For model fit, the results of the omnibus likelihood ratio test and the Wald tests for contribution of each IV in the model should be preferred. Nonetheless, in some research

TABLE 4.6

Classification Table for Full CO Model, $N = 3,365$

	Predcat0	Predcat1	Predcat2	Predcat3	Predcat4	Predcat5	Totals
profread							
0	**0**	1	9	57	0	0	67
1	1	**2**	12	262	0	1	278
2	0	3	**24**	565	0	2	594
3	1	3	24	**1,428**	0	26	1,482
4	0	1	1	577	**0**	8	587
5	0	0	0	332	0	**25**	357
Totals	2	10	70	3,221	0	62	3,365

situations, reliability in classification may be an important component of model selection criteria; this example demonstrates how these statistics are calculated, as well as how much they can be influenced by group sample size.

Assumption of Proportional
Odds and Linearity in the Logit

Within an ordinal model, linearity in the logit cannot be assessed directly, and "only if linear relations between the logits and the covariates are established in the separate binary logistic models [is] a check of the proportional odds assumption . . . meaningful" (Bender & Grouven, 1998, p. 814). Thus, this assumption was investigated for each of the five binary models to provide support for the ordinal model. Linearity in the logit was examined for the continuous variables using the Box-Tidwell method (Hosmer & Lemeshow, 1989; Menard, 1995) and by graphical methods (Bender & Grouven, 1998). For Box-Tidwell, multiplicative terms of the form $X \times \ln(X)$ are created for the continuous explanatory variables and added to the main effects models. Statistically significant interaction terms are an indication that linearity may not be a reasonable assumption for that variable. To look at linearity graphically, deciles can be created for the continuous explanatory variables, then plotted against the proportion of children in the "success" category for each binary logit (at or beyond category j). Both approaches were taken for the two continuous variables in the models looked at here: age at kindergarten entry (*p1ageent*) and family SES (*wksesl*). The graphs revealed a linear trend, but the Box-Tidwell method indicated nonlinearity for the two continuous variables in all five binary logits. Given the graphical pattern, large sample size, and sensitivity of the statistical tests, linearity in the logit was assumed plausible for both continuous variables.

For the full CO model, the score test for the assumption of proportional or parallel odds was rejected. This means that there are some independent variables for which the odds of being at or beyond category j are not stable across proficiency levels as j changes. Table 4.7 (values have been rounded to save space) provides the results of five separate binary logistic regressions, where the data were dichotomized and analyzed according to the pattern in the second CO column of Table 4.1. That is, each logistic model looks at the probability of being at or beyond proficiency level j. For these logistic models (using SPSS), the grouping of categories coded 1 corresponds to children who were at or beyond each successive category, and the code of 0 is used for children below each successive category.

Reviewing the results of the separate logistic models in Table 4.7, relative to the results of the CO model in Table 4.5, we see that all five binary models fit the data well. The model χ^2's are all statistically significant, indicating that each model fits better relative to its corresponding null model; and the H-L tests are all not statistically significant, indicating that observed to predicted probabilities are consistent.

Now let us look at the patterns of slopes and ORs for each explanatory variable across these five models. The effect of *gender*, after adjusting for the other independent variables, does seem to have a dissimilar pattern across the five separate logistic regression splits. Although the average *gender* slope for these five regressions is −.604, which is somewhat close to the *gender* slope from the multivariable CO model (−.500), the odds ratio for boys to girls of being at or beyond proficiency level 1 (.354) are somewhat lower relative to the other four comparisons (.552, .625, .631, and .635, respectively). Note, however, that if we compare the OR for the averaged *gender* slopes from these binary models, exp(−.604) = .547, to the single *gender* OR from the CO model of .607, we see little difference, *on average*. Directionally and on average, the effect of gender is similar across the five logistic regressions. This is true for all the explanatory variables in the model, with the exception of the effect of *minority*. Notice that the direction of the effect of *minority* changes between the first three analyses and the last two. In the first three analyses, the odds are less than 1.0, suggesting that minority children, relative to nonminority children, are more likely to be in the lower proficiency categories. However, there is no difference in the likelihood of being at or beyond proficiency category 4, because the OR is not statistically different from 1.0. The last analysis compares children in categories 0 through 4 with children in category 5. Here we see that minority children are *more likely* than nonminority children to be in category 5 ($b = .238$, OR = 1.268) after adjusting for the presence of the other explanatory variables in the model. This result was not apparent through the cumulative odds model. The CO model provides summary estimates of the effect

TABLE 4.7

Associated Cumulative Binary Models for the CO Analysis (Descending),
Where $CUMSP_j$ Compares $Y < $ cat. j to $Y \geq$ cat. j, $N = 3{,}365$

Variable	$CUMSP_1$ b $(se(b))$ OR	$CUMSP_2$ b $(se(b))$ OR	$CUMSP_3$ b $(se(b))$ OR	$CUMSP_4$ b $(se(b))$ OR	$CUMSP_5$ b $(se(b))$ OR	Score Test[a] p value
Constant	3.53 (2.11)	−.55 (.99)	−2.15** (.68)	−4.67** (.68)	−7.34** (.99)	
gender	−1.04 (.28) .35*	−.60 (.12) .55*	−.47 (.08) .63*	−.46 (.08) .63*	−.46 (.12) .64*	.249
famrisk	−.15 (.29) .87	−.25 (.13) .78	−.21 (.09) .81*	−.33 (.10) .72*	−.28 (.15) .76	.450
center	−.03 (.28) .97	−.10 (.14) .91	.10 (.09) 1.10	.10 (.10) 1.10	.26 (.16) 1.30	.219
noreadbo	−.65 (.27) .52*	−.36 (.14) .70*	−.28 (.10) .75*	−.28 (.12) .76*	−.50 (.21) .61*	.095
minority	−.23 (.29) .80	−.42 (.13) .66*	−.39 (.09) .68*	.09 (.09) 1.09	.24 (.13) 1.27*	**.000**
halfdayK	.07 (.26) .93	−.00 (.12) 1.00	−.11 (.08) .89	−.26 (.08) .77*	−.11 (.12) .89	.033
wksesl	1.00 (.17) 2.73*	.77 (.10) 2.17*	.73 (.07) 2.07*	.64 (.06) 1.89*	.87 (.08) 2.39*	**.000**
plageent	.02 (.03) 1.03	.05 (.02) 1.06*	.06 (.01) 1.06*	.06 (.01) 1.06*	.08 (.02) 1.08*	.645
R^2_L	.125	.097	.092	.070	.096	
R^2_N	.136	.128	.149	.115	.128	
Model χ^2_8	82.11**	215.49**	366.40**	280.39**	217.92**	
H-L[b] χ^2_8	7.80	10.43	13.41	.74	9.16	

a. Score test for each IV, unadjusted (no other covariates in the model).
b. Hosmer-Lemeshow test, all n.s.
*$p < .05$; **$p < .01$.

of a variable across all cumulative proficiency-level dichotomizations or splits to the data. The imposition of the assumption of proportionality of the odds across these splits does not seem to be valid for the *minority* variable. For all other explanatory variables in the model, the direction and average magnitude of the slopes and the ORs corresponds well to the CO results.

Unfortunately, the score test for the proportional odds assumption is very sensitive to sample size and the number of different possible covariate patterns, which will always be very large when continuous explanatory variables are used. If the assumption is not rejected, the researcher should feel confident that the overall CO model represents the pattern of ORs across the separate cumulative splits very well. If the assumption is not upheld, however, good practice dictates that the separate models be fit and compared with the CO results to check for discrepancies or deviations from the general pattern suggested by the CO model (e.g., Allison, 1999; Bender & Grouven, 1998; Brant, 1990; Clogg & Shihadeh, 1994; Long, 1997; O'Connell, 2000).

To provide an additional check on the plausibility of the proportionality assumption, separate score tests unadjusted for the presence of the other covariates in the cumulative odds model can be reviewed for each of the explanatory variables. In light of the large sample size, a .01 level of significance was used to guide decisions regarding nonproportionality. For each of the single binary models, the score test for the assumption of proportional odds was upheld, with the exception of *minority* and family SES (*wksesl*). The *p* values for these unadjusted tests are presented in the final column of Table 4.7. Across the five binary logit models, the ORs for *wksesl* are approximately 1.9 or larger, indicating that higher-SES children are at least twice as likely as lower-SES children to be in the higher proficiency categories. Given the fact that SES is continuous, the magnitude of the difference in ORs across the binary splits seems to be negligible and as such, a common OR may be a reasonable assumption for this variable. As mentioned above, however, the pattern of change in the ORs for the *minority* variable may clearly be relevant to the study of proficiency, and the effects of this variable should be examined more closely. Although not provided here, follow-up analyses including interactions among the predictors or using a variable for separate categories of race/ethnicity rather than an overall assignment to a minority category could be used to better explain the effects seen in the five binary logit models.

Alternatives to the Cumulative Odds Model

Recall that the best use of the cumulative odds model is to provide for a single parsimonious prediction model for the data. However, if the restriction of equal slopes is not realistic, it is incumbent upon the researcher to work toward explaining how the data are behaving rather than forcing the data to conform to a particular model. There are several alternatives available if, after review of the separate logistic regression analyses and checks on linearity and proportionality, the overall assumption of proportionality in the multivariate ordinal model is deemed suspect.

If variable effects are of primary importance, the researcher may decide to work with the separate logistic regressions to explore and explain divergent explanatory variable patterns across the different cumulative models (Bender & Grouven, 1998). This decision depends on the researcher's overall goals for the analysis and clearly may not be appropriate for every situation or research question. If a parsimonious model or a single set of predicted probabilities is desired, these separate binary logits will not provide it. Alternatively, the researcher may decide to forfeit the ordinal nature of the DV altogether and to fit a multinomial model to the data. This approach may provide some meaningful information in terms of overall variable effects and classification, but it neglects the ordinal nature of the outcome and thus disregards an important aspect of the data. This option, too, may not be optimal for the researcher's goal, but it should be considered if the researcher believes that the majority of the explanatory variables are contributing to the violation of the proportional odds assumption. See Borooah (2002), Ishii-Kuntz (1994), and Agresti (1990, 1996) for examples and discussion of these alternative multinomial approaches.

A third option, and the focus of later chapters in this book, is to consider other types of ordinal regression analyses, such as the continuation ratio method or the adjacent categories method, to try and obtain a single well-fitting and parsimonious model that would aid in our understanding of the data at hand. Chapter 5 demonstrates the use of the CR or continuation ratio model, and Chapter 6 presents the AC or adjacent categories model.

Before turning to a discussion of these additional strategies for analyzing ordered outcomes, one additional method will be presented. In situations where proportionality is questionable based on the behavior of only a subset of the explanatory variables, researchers may opt to fit what are called *partial proportional odds* (PPO) models (Ananth & Kleinbaum, 1997; Koch et al., 1985; Peterson & Harrell, 1990). In essence, PPO models allow for an interaction between an independent variable and the different logit comparisons, which clarifies how the odds for an IV may change across the levels of the outcomes being compared. SAS currently estimates PPO models using PROC GENMOD. The analysis requires data restructuring to reflect whether or not an individual is at or beyond a particular response level (Stokes, Davis, & Koch, 2000). In the restructured data set, a new binary response for each person for each ordered logit comparison is created to indicate whether or not that person is at or beyond each particular response level. For example, with a K-category ordinal response variable, each person would have $K - 1$ lines in the restructured data set. The new outcome variable of interest is derived to indicate, for each of the $K - 1$ logits, whether or not the person was at or beyond category K (excluding the lowest category ($Y = 0$), which all children are at or beyond). Because the data are now correlated (repeated observations among persons), generalized estimating equations (GEE) are used to fit the nonproportional model and then the partial proportional odds model. The use of the GEE approach (Liang & Zeger, 1986) is particularly well suited to the study of repeated measurements over time when the outcomes of interest are categorical (nominal or ordinal). It is based on large-sample properties, which means that the sample size has to be sufficient enough to produce reliable estimates. Stokes et al. (2000) suggest that two-way cross-classifications of the data should yield observed counts of at least five. With continuous explanatory variables, this typically will not be the case, so the sample size should be considered carefully.

EXAMPLE 4.3: Partial Proportional Odds

Using the ECLS-K example to demonstrate, we can release the assumption of proportional odds for the *minority* variable and refit the model in an attempt to better reflect the pattern seen in Table 4.7. That is, the assumption of proportional odds is retained for all variables in the model except for *minority*. The syntax for the PPO model, including the restructuring of the data set, is included in Appendix B5, following the process outlined by Stokes et al. (2000). Figure 4.2 presents the (edited) printout for this analysis. GENMOD models the probability that a child is at or beyond category j, but because the odds ratios are kept constant across all splits for each variable except *minority*, the results include only one intercept parameter. The threshold values are found by adding the estimates for each corresponding split, which are included toward the middle of the "Analysis of GEE Parameter Estimates" table in Figure 4.2. When reviewing this table, note that the explanatory variable coding scheme uses the "0" category for the categorical variables as the referent. For example, the slope for *gender*, $b = .5002$, is provided for girls (*gender* = 0) rather than for boys (*gender* = 1).

The intercept (-6.9805) is the log-odds that a child would be at or beyond proficiency category 5 ($Y \geq 5$) if all his or her covariate scores were 1, or 0 if continuous; note that the coding of categorical variables follows an internally constructed pattern and that the estimate for split 5 is 0.00. To find the log-odds for $Y \geq 4$, the threshold would be the intercept plus the effect for split 4 ($-6.9805 + 1.2670 = -5.7135$). The other threshold estimates may be found similarly.

The GEE analysis provides a score statistic for testing the contribution of each explanatory variable to the model; these are found at the end of the output. Results of the score tests indicate that the effect of *minority* for the fifth logit comparison is just marginally statistically significant, $\chi^2_1 = 4.04$, $p = .0445$, yet its interaction with the split variable is strongly significant overall, $\chi^2_4 = 28.80$, $p < .0001$. This result suggests that there are reliable differences in the effect of *minority* depending on split. For the other explanatory variables in the model, all effects are statistically significant except attendance at a daycare center (*center*), consistent with what was found in the full cumulative odds model. GENMOD also provides z tests (the normal distribution version of the Wald statistic) for the contribution of explanatory variables in the model; these are found in the "Analysis of GEE Parameter Estimates" table of Figure 4.2. Results of the z tests are consistent with the score tests, with the exception of *minority*.

Given the interaction between *minority* and split, the effect for *minority* is interpreted via the score test that specifically examines its contribution for the fifth cumulative comparison. For each of the other splits, the z tests for the *minority* × split interactions contained in the model suggest that there is no difference in the odds for minority versus nonminority children for the first cumulative comparison ($Y \geq 1$), $b_{int.1} = .5077$, $p = .0677$, nor for the fourth ($Y \geq 4$), $b_{int.4} = .0282$, $p = .7884$. Substantively, these findings are consistent with those of the separate binary models in Table 4.7. There, *minority* had no statistical effect on the individual cumulative logits either for the first binary model ($p > .05$) or for the fourth ($p > .05$).

The *minority* × split interactions inform us as to how much change occurs in the effect of *minority* across the thresholds of the response variable. With the assumption of proportional odds relaxed for *minority*, the results shown in the printout tell us how much the log-odds are expected to change for nonminority children relative to minority children, across the different logistic regression splits. For example, after adjusting for the other covariates in the model, the odds ratio for a nonminority child relative to a minority child for a proficiency score at or beyond category 5 is exp($-.1560$) = .855; the odds ratio for a minority child relative to a nonminority child for a proficiency score at or beyond category 5 is then exp($+.1560$) = 1.169. This OR can be compared with Table 4.7 for the fifth cumulative logistic regression split (where OR = 1.268). Further, this OR is statistically different from 1.0 in the PPO model ($p = .0445$ in "Score Statistics For Type 3 GEE Analysis" table), as it is in the fifth cumulative comparison based on the separate binary models ($p < .05$ for last split in Table 4.7).

```
The GENMOD Procedure

                          Model Information

                  Data Set              WORK.PPOM
                  Distribution          Binomial
                  Link Function         Logit
                  Dependent Variable    beyond
                  Observations Used     16825



                       Class Level Information

Class      Levels   Values

split        5       1 2 3 4 5
GENDER       2       0 1
FAMRISK      2       0.00 1.00
CENTER       2       0.00 1.00
NOREADBO     2       0.00 1.00
MINORITY     2       0.00 1.00
HALFDAYK     2       0.00 1.00
CHILDID    3365       0212014C 0294004C 3035008C 3042008C 3042023C
                      0044007C 0195025C 0243009C 0621012C 0748011C
                      0832023C 3041005C 0028009C 0028014C 0052003C
                      0052007C 0195020C 0196007C 0196016C 0196017C
                      0196018C 0212002C 0212012C 0216006C 0220005C
                      0220020C 0301002C 0301004C ...



                          Response Profile

                  Ordered                  Total
                  Value       beyond     Frequency

                    1           1          10045
                    2           0           6780

PROC GENMOD is modeling the probability that beyond='1'.



              Criteria For Assessing Goodness Of Fit

   Criterion                 DF          Value      Value/DF
   Deviance                 17E3      12003.9325      0.7142
   Scaled Deviance          17E3      12003.9325      0.7142
   Pearson Chi-Square       17E3      16074.6352      0.9564
   Scaled Pearson X2        17E3      16074.6352      0.9564
   Log Likelihood                     -6001.9662
```

Figure 4.2   Partial Proportional Odds for Minority: GEE Analysis

Figure 4.2 (Continued)

```
                    Analysis Of GEE Parameter Estimates
                    Empirical Standard Error Estimates

                               Standard   95% Confidence
Parameter                Estimate  Error      Limits        Z Pr > |Z|

Intercept                 -6.9805  0.5753  -8.1081  -5.8528  -12.13  <.0001
GENDER           0         0.5002  0.0663   0.3703   0.6301    7.55  <.0001
GENDER           1         0.0000  0.0000   0.0000   0.0000      .      .
FAMRISK          0.00      0.2596  0.0778   0.1071   0.4120    3.34  0.0008
FAMRISK          1.00      0.0000  0.0000   0.0000   0.0000      .      .
CENTER           0.00     -0.0759  0.0770  -0.2268   0.0750   -0.99  0.3240
CENTER           1.00      0.0000  0.0000   0.0000   0.0000      .      .
NOREADBO         0.00      0.3366  0.0913   0.1575   0.5156    3.68  0.0002
NOREADBO         1.00      0.0000  0.0000   0.0000   0.0000      .
MINORITY         0.00     -0.1560  0.1240  -0.3989   0.0870   -1.26  0.2083
MINORITY         1.00      0.0000  0.0000   0.0000   0.0000      .      .
HALFDAYK         0.00      0.1451  0.0666   0.0145   0.2757    2.18  0.0295
HALFDAYK         1.00      0.0000  0.0000   0.0000   0.0000      .      .
WKSESL                     0.7450  0.0514   0.6442   0.8457   14.49  <.0001
P1AGEENT                   0.0588  0.0084   0.0423   0.0753    7.00  <.0001
split            1         6.2595  0.1851   5.8968   6.6223   33.82  <.0001
split            2         4.4067  0.1204   4.1707   4.6428   36.59  <.0001
split            3         3.0966  0.1043   2.8923   3.3010   29.70  <.0001
split            4         1.2670  0.0846   1.1012   1.4328   14.98  <.0001
split            5         0.0000  0.0000   0.0000   0.0000      .      .
split*MINORITY 1 0.00      0.5077  0.2779  -0.0370   1.0523    1.83  0.0677
split*MINORITY 1 1.00      0.0000  0.0000   0.0000   0.0000      .      .
split*MINORITY 2 0.00      0.6021  0.1621   0.2843   0.9198    3.71  0.0002
split*MINORITY 2 1.00      0.0000  0.0000   0.0000   0.0000      .      .
split*MINORITY 3 0.00      0.5230  0.1334   0.2615   0.7844    3.92  <.0001
split*MINORITY 3 1.00      0.0000  0.0000   0.0000   0.0000      .      .
split*MINORITY 4 0.00      0.0282  0.1050  -0.1777   0.2340    0.27  0.7884
split*MINORITY 4 1.00      0.0000  0.0000   0.0000   0.0000      .      .
split*MINORITY 5 0.00      0.0000  0.0000   0.0000   0.0000      .      .
split*MINORITY 5 1.00      0.0000  0.0000   0.0000   0.0000      .      .


              Score Statistics For Type 3 GEE Analysis

                                   Chi-
            Source          DF    Square     Pr > ChiSq

            GENDER           1     57.02       <.0001
            FAMRISK          1     11.10       0.0009
            CENTER           1      0.97       0.3243
            NOREADBO         1     13.30       0.0003
            MINORITY         1      4.04       0.0445
            HALFDAYK         1      4.75       0.0294
            WKSESL           1    195.03       <.0001
            P1AGEENT         1     49.02       <.0001
            split            4   2447.16       <.0001
            split*MINORITY   4     28.80       <.0001
```

To find the effect of *minority* for the fourth cumulative logit, $(Y \geq 4)$, the interaction terms are added to the main effect. That is, for the odds of a nonminority child being at or beyond category 4, $\exp(-.1560 + .0282) = \exp(-.1278) = .880$; for minority children, this corresponds to $\exp(+.1278) = 1.136$. Minority children are 1.136 times as likely to be at or beyond category 4, although this effect is not statistically different from 1.0 $(p = .7884)$. This effect is consistent with the OR for the fourth cumulative logit in Table 4.7, which also was not statistically significant (OR = 1.092, not significant). For the first logit, $(Y \geq 1)$, the effect for nonminority children is $\exp(-.1560 + .5077) = \exp(.3517) = 1.42$; for minority children, the effect is $\exp(-.3517) = .7035$. According to the PPO model, this effect is not significant $(p = .0677)$, consistent with the result for the effect of *minority* at this first split in Table 4.7 (OR = .796, not significant). Overall, minority children are less likely than their nonminority peers to advance beyond proficiency levels 2 and 3, but given that they have attained at least proficiency level 4, they are more likely than their nonminority peers to then achieve mastery in proficiency level 5.

To examine the effects of the explanatory variables for which the proportional odds assumption was retained, the slope estimates can be interpreted directly. For the effect of *gender*, girls (*gender* = 0) are $\exp(+.5002) = 1.65$ times as likely as boys to be at or beyond level 1, after adjusting for other covariates in the model, and this OR remains constant across all underlying cumulative logits. Because the events for this explanatory variable with only two levels are complementary, we can easily interpret the effect for boys as well: boys are $\exp(-.5002) = .606$ times as likely as girls to be at or beyond a given proficiency category j, after adjusting for other covariates. For all explanatory variables with the exception of *minority*, the effects are equivalent to those presented for the full CO model in Table 4.5, once the coding of IVs is taken into account. For example, in the full CO model the gender slope is $-.500$ with OR = .607. Variable effects in the PPO model for those variables for which the proportional odds assumption was retained are of the same magnitude and statistical significance as those in the CO model. The direction has changed because SAS PROC GENMOD provides the estimates for the values of the explanatory variable coded as 0 rather than 1. Note that the nature of the coding for the categorical IVs does not affect the results for the continuous variables in the model between the CO and PPO models.

To summarize the PPO analysis, this approach does resolve some of the issues surrounding the full proportional odds model, particularly for the *minority* variable. The GEE estimates correspond quite well with the separate effects for minority that were examined across the binary logit models in terms of both magnitude and statistical significance. In the study of early reading achievement, this result bears further investigation. Creating a variable that categorizes groupings of children based on race/ethnicity for inclusion in these models rather than including all "nonwhite" children together in a dichotomous arrangement should be further examined, but this is not the focus of the current demonstration. The effects for the variables that were constrained to follow the proportional odds assumption were found to be consistent with the earlier CO analysis. There is currently no overall summary measure of goodness of fit for a GEE analysis provided through GENMOD (Stokes et al., 2000), but the criteria included in the output under the "Criteria for Assessing Goodness of Fit" heading indicate that the deviance (found through a comparison between the fitted model and the perfect, or saturated, model) is less than its degrees of freedom (value/df) < 1.0), suggestive of adequate model fit (Allison, 1999). Recall that there is no reliable test of the model deviance when continuous variables are present. However, these statistics can be useful for comparisons of competing models. Overall, the PPO model seems to be more informative than the CO model, particularly with regard to the explanatory variable of *minority*.

5. THE CONTINUATION RATIO MODEL

Overview of the Continuation Ratio Model

As we saw in Chapter 4, the cumulative odds model uses all the data available to assess the effect of independent variables on the log-odds of being *at or beyond* (or the reverse, *at or below*) a particular category. The odds are found by considering the probability of being *at or beyond* a category relative to the probability of being *below* that category. A restrictive assumption made in the CO analysis is that across all cumulative logit comparisons, the effect of any independent variable is similar; that is, the odds of being in higher categories relative to being in *any* category below it remains constant across the categories. However, these logit comparisons for the cumulative odds may not be theoretically appropriate in every research situation. If interest lies in determining the effects of independent variables on the event of being in a higher stage or category, then a comparison group that includes *all* people who failed to make it to a category may not lead us to the best conclusions or understanding of the data in terms of differences between people at a low stage versus all higher stages. Rather than grouping together all people who failed to make it to a category at any point, an alternative ordinal approach involves comparisons between respondents in any given category versus all those who achieved a higher category score. This approach forms the class of models known as continuation ratio (CR) models. The focus of a CR analysis is to understand the factors that distinguish between those persons who have reached a particular response level but do not move on from those persons who do advance to a higher level. Fox (1997) refers to this process as the analysis of a series of "nested dichotomies" (p. 472).

A continuation ratio is a *conditional* probability. The discussion to follow explains how these continuation ratios can be formed in different ways, depending on the researcher's goals. The examples presented are based on continuation ratios that take the form δ_j = P(response beyond cat. j|response in at least cat. j), or its complement, $1 - \delta_j$ = P(response in cat. j|response in at least cat. j).

Armstrong and Sloan (1989), McCullagh and Nelder (1983), Greenland (1994), and Agresti (1990, 1996) have discussed the continuation ratio model in depth and have highlighted the relationship between the CR model and the proportional hazards model proposed by D. R. Cox (1972). The proportional hazards model is a familiar one in epidemiological contexts and in the survival analysis research literature, but its value can be extended to other contexts as well.

The CR models can be fit using a suitably restructured data set with either a logit link function or a complementary log-log (clog-log) link function. The restructuring is explained in greater detail later, but essentially, a new data set is created from $K - 1$ smaller data sets, in which each person has as many data lines as his or her outcome score allows. The process is similar to how the concatenated data set was created for the partial proportional odds analysis, with the very important exception that inclusion in a data set is conditional on whether or not mastery was attained at a particular level. The resulting data sets then correspond to the specific comparisons contained in Table 4.1 for the continuation ratio analyses. Once the data set is concatenated, the outcome of interest is on whether or not a child advances beyond a particular category, given that at least mastery in that category was attained. The data sets formed in this fashion are conditionally independent (Armstrong & Sloan, 1989; Clogg & Shihadeh, 1994; Fox, 1997); thus, the restructured data set can be analyzed using statistical methods for binary outcomes.

The restructuring is necessary in order to derive the desired conditional probabilities, or, in the case of the clog-log link, the hazards. In the epidemiological literature, the hazard ratio is also known as relative risk; it is a ratio of two hazards, where the hazard is an explicit conditional probability. The odds ratio, on the other hand, is a ratio of two odds, where the odds are a quotient of complementary probabilities, $p/(1 - p)$. Of course, the probability of interest in a logit model could be a conditional probability, which clarifies the usefulness of the logit link for continuation ratio models. As we shall see in the examples to follow, the two link functions share some important similarities, but structurally they are very different.

The first approach, using the logit link, has been called the "logistic continuation ratio model" (Greenland, 1994, p. 1668). The model treats *time to an event* as a discrete quantity. It is not necessary for the ordinal outcome Y to be a timed variable, as the following discussion will make clear. For the ECLS-K first-grade data, this "time" can be conceptualized as measured for each person at each of the six levels of the outcome. Let the $K = 6$ response categories represent the possible "times" for the event of being *beyond* category j to occur. Then each person has at most $K - 1 = 5$ opportunities for the event to occur (because no one in the sample based on a discrete ordinal outcome is observed to be *beyond* the final category). At each time and for each person, either the event of interest, being *beyond* category j, has occurred or it has not occurred. Two new variables are created: time, which can also be called "level" or "stage", and the outcome, which in the discussion below is called "beyond": Either the child advances beyond a specific level (1), or the child does not advance beyond a specific level (0). With a simple restructuring of the data set (presented below) and the use of the logit link, the results of this approach are conceptually similar to, and thus an approximation for, the discrete proportional hazards model. The CR model using the logit link provides the odds for a child of being beyond a particular category, conditional on being at or beyond that category. Similar to the cumulative odds model, the logistic CR model assumes that the slopes are homogeneous across the separate nested binary models that could be used to represent the data (as in Table 4.1). In this context, the restriction is referred to as the equal slopes or parallel odds assumption.

The second approach considers time to the event as a continuous quantity. In this case, the complementary log-log link is used on the restructured data set, and the model provides "estimates of an underlying proportional hazards model in continuous time" (Allison, 1995, p. 212). The model assumes that the hazards, rather than the odds, are parallel across the levels of the outcome variable. Similar to the proportional odds assumption, the parallel slopes (or hazards) assumption implies that the effect of an explanatory variable is assumed constant across the outcome categories.

The proportional hazards model is particularly useful when the response variable is ordinal, because the variable effects estimated from a grouped continuous model, for which the previously reviewed cumulative odds model is an example, are equivalent to the estimated effects in a continuation ratio model when the complementary log-log link is used (Läärä & Matthews, 1985; McCullagh & Nelder, 1989). Bender and Benner (2000) define the class of grouped continuous models as follows:

The name "grouped continuous model" can be explained by the view that Y is a discretized variable of an underlying latent continuous trait defined by cut-off points j. It is then natural to formulate a model by means of the cumulative probabilities g_j. It is, however, not essentially necessary to suppose the existence of an underlying continuous variable in order to use the cumulative probabilities for the description of the ordinal categories. (p. 680)

Link Functions

Chapter 3 described the link function in terms of the process of "linking" a transformation of the observed responses to the original data. For the logit link, we first considered the outcomes in terms of probability of one of the categories, which we called "success." Next, we formed the odds of success, and our final transformation involved taking the log of these odds. Letting $\pi(\underline{x})$ represent the probability of success given a set of covariates $\underline{x}$, the logit link function can be written as $g(y) = \ln[(\pi(\underline{x})/(1 - \pi(\underline{x}))]$. We fit a linear model based on this link function such that the logits for the success response are predicted: $g(y) = \alpha + \beta_1 X_{i1} + \beta_2 X_{i2} + \ldots \beta_p X_{ip}$. The logistic distribution is the inverse of this process if the logit link is used, so that $\pi(\underline{x}) = \exp(g(y))/[1 + \exp(g(y))]$, and thus the logistic regression model provides the estimates for the original probabilities of success or failure. The logit link is often favored over other link functions because of its simplicity in interpretation of results in terms of odds and odds ratios.

The logistic distribution function provides a reasonable assessment of the relationship between the independent variables and the dichotomous outcome, but it is not the only distribution that can be used. For binomial data, other equally valid link functions and corresponding distributions include the probit link function and its inverse, the cumulative standard normal distribution, and the complementary log-log function and its inverse, the extreme value distribution. Fox (1997) provides a brief description of these transformations, but the interested reader should also consult Borooah (2002) and McCullagh and Nelder (1989) for detailed information about these and other link options.

The complementary log-log link function models the transformed response in the following way: $g(y) = \log(-\log(1 - \pi(\underline{x})))$, where $\pi(\underline{x})$ represents a "success" probability for a given set of covariates. In a continuation ratio model, $\pi(\underline{x})$ is a conditional probability; that is, $\pi(\underline{x})$ represents the probability that a person moves beyond a stage once a particular stage has been reached, or its complement, the probability that a person does not move beyond a stage once a particular stage has been reached. The linear model based on this transformation is $g(y) = \alpha + \beta_1 X_{i1} + \beta_2 X_{i2} + \ldots \beta_p X_{ip}$.

The inverse of this process, if the clog-log link is used, is the extreme value distribution, so that $\pi(\underline{x}) = 1 - \exp(-\exp(g(y)))$.

Probabilities of Interest

The probabilities of interest for the CR model are the probabilities of being *beyond* any category, given that a person has already attained at least that specific category, $\delta_j = P(Y_i > \text{cat. } j | Y_i \geq \text{cat. } j)$. These continuation ratios are *conditional* probabilities, rather than cumulative probabilities, and the process of predicting the conditional probabilities is different in form from the process used in the CO model. In particular, as j increases, all cases with responses less than j are dropped out of the model for each logit comparison. Note that the complement of δ_j, $1 - \delta_j$, is equal to $1 - P(Y_i > \text{cat. } j | Y_i \geq \text{cat. } j) = P(Y_i = \text{cat. } j | Y_i \geq \text{cat. } j)$. This is essentially the probability being sought through the proportional hazards model. If time is continuous and we are interested in modeling the time to the occurrence of an event, denoted by T, the hazard rate describes the probability of T occurring in any interval (which can be quite small), given that T has not yet occurred. As presented by Allison (1995), the hazard is found by taking the limit of this probability:

$$h(t) = \lim_{\Delta t \to 0} \frac{P(t \leq T \leq t + \Delta t | T \geq t)}{\Delta t}.$$

In a sense, this limit converges on $P(T = t | T \geq t)$, which is why the hazard is sometimes referred to as a failure rate. Tabachnick and Fidell (2001) describe the hazard, or failure, rate as "the rate of not surviving to the midpoint of an interval, given survival to the start of the interval" (p. 779). In the context of an ordinal outcome, survival implies moving beyond a particular level j given that level j was reached; not surviving implies that the person stops at a particular response category j and therefore does not advance, given that level j was reached. Instead of survival times, we have survival events—either the person advances beyond category j or the person doesn't, given that category j was reached. Those individuals not reaching category j would have failed earlier and thus would not be included in the probability calculations beyond their last stage attained. These estimated probabilities can be found directly using the continuation ratio model.

To develop continuation ratio models, the data must be restructured to reflect, for each person, whether or not there is survival at each of the levels of the response variable. Consequently, the development of CR models using the logit link or the clog-log link is consistent with the approach of

59

the proportional hazards model. The probabilities obtained through the logit link model estimate the conditional probability of "surviving," that is, advancing to a higher stage on the early reading continuum, given that *at least* that particular mastery level has been attained. When the clog-log link function is applied on the same restructured data set, the analysis is equivalent to the discrete-time proportional hazards model (Allison, 1999). For the ECLS-K data, probabilities obtained through the clog-log link model on the restructured data set are also conditional probabilities, estimating the probability of *not* advancing to a higher stage along the early reading skills continuum level, given that mastery *at least* at a given level was attained. As the examples to follow will illustrate, model slope estimates using the clog-log link are also equivalent to the slope estimates when the clog-log link is used on the original data set for the cumulative odds analysis (Läärä & Matthews, 1985).

Directionality of Responses and Formation of the Continuation Ratios

Before considering some examples, it is important to be aware of the selected directional coding of the ordinal outcome, as this decision becomes critical in the continuation ratio approach. The coding itself is completely up to the researcher, and in that regard it is arbitrary as long as consistency in direction is maintained. For example, the numbers 0, 1, 2, . . . 5 have been used to indicate whether or not mastery of early reading skills (Table 2.1) was obtained. The reverse also could have been used, with 0 representing attainment of mastery at level 5, and 5 representing inability to master the level 1 skills. Earlier, we saw that with the cumulative odds model, the interpretation of results remains exactly the same under a reversal of the coding scheme, although the direction of the slopes representing each effect is reversed within the model (e.g., instead of *gender* having a slope of –.500 in the full CO logit model (Table 4.5), it would have had a slope of +.500 if the outcome values were used in reverse order). The use of the ascending versus descending option in SAS changes only the outcome of interest being modeled (e.g., in the CO model we would have $P(Y \geq \text{cat. } j)$ rather than $P(Y \leq \text{cat. } j)$ if the descending option is used). In the CO model, variable effects are invariant as to how the outcome is coded. However, when we start to consider the estimation of conditional probabilities, the models we derive and their interpretations explicitly depend on the manner in which the ordinal outcome is coded— either increasing or decreasing. As long as the careful analyst is aware of the questions he or she wants to ask of the data, and correctly sets up the coding of the ordinal outcome to correspond to those questions, there should be no confusion. In the examples that follow, this correspondence should be made clear.

There are several unique ways that continuation ratio models might be constructed. Typically, these are referred to as "forward CR" or "backward CR" (Bender & Benner, 2000; Clogg & Shihadeh, 1994; Hosmer & Lemeshow, 2000). These characterizations are not obtained by simply reversing the order of the outcome categories, because the CR models are not invariant to reversal of the outcome codes (Allison, 1999; Greenland, 1994). The models presented here use the forward approach, which corresponds naturally to the process of progression through the six hierarchically structured early reading skill categories. In particular, interest lies in modeling the probability that the ith child would advance beyond a particular category, given that he or she achieved mastery at least for that category. For a collection of explanatory variables, $\underline{x}$, the probabilities of interest are $P(Y_i > \text{cat. } j | Y_i \geq \text{cat. } j, \underline{x})$. Note that the complement of this event for each category is $1 - P(Y_i > \text{cat. } j | Y_i \geq \text{cat. } j, \underline{x}) = P(Y_i = \text{cat. } j | Y_i \geq \text{cat. } j, \underline{x})$. Later, it will be shown how this particular construction of the forward continuation ratios is consistent with the results of an analysis using the clog-log link on the original data.

EXAMPLE 5.1: Continuation Ratio Model With Logit Link and Restructuring the Data

For the ECLS-K first-grade example, we will first reconsider the original data in terms of these conditional probabilities, provided in Table 5.1, for the single explanatory variable of *gender*. I will let the desired probability, $P(Y_i > \text{cat. } j | Y_i \geq \text{cat. } j, \underline{x})$, be denoted by δ_j, where $j = 0, 1, \ldots 5$. The odds of being beyond a particular category, given proficiency in that category or higher, are found by calculating $\delta_j / (1 - \delta_j)$. From Table 5.1, we see that for both boys and girls, the conditional probability, δ_j, of advancing beyond any particular proficiency level generally decreases across categories, although δ_j increases slightly for boys between categories 3 and 4. Overall, as greater mastery for early literacy skills is achieved, children are less likely to advance to higher categories. For boys, the likelihood of advancing is always less than that for girls. The odds for boys and girls, shown in Table 5.1, correspond to these observed conditional probability patterns. For these data, the odds that a girl advances, conditional on the event that she has attained a given level of proficiency, are always greater than the corresponding odds for boys. The OR (boys to girls) for these data across the categories do not appear to be similar. The

TABLE 5.1

Observed ECLS-K Gender Frequency (f), Category
Probability (p), and Conditional Probabilities
P(Beyond Category j Given at Least Category j) (δ_j)

	Category						
	0	1	2	3	4	5	Totals (f)
Males							
f	48	163	320	735	256	151	1673
p	.0278	.0974	.1913	.4393	.1530	.0903	1.000
δ_j	.9713	.8997	.7811	.3564	.3710	—	—
$1 - \delta_j$	.0287	.1003	.2189	.6436	.6290	—	—
Females							
f	19	115	274	747	331	206	1692
p	.0112	.0680	.1619	.4415	.1956	.1217	1.000
δ_j	.9888	.9313	.8241	.4182	.3836	—	—
$1 - \delta_j$	.0112	.0687	.1759	.5818	.6164	—	—
Odds							
Males	33.84	8.970	3.568	.5538	.5898		
Females	88.286	13.556	4.685	.7188	.6223		
OR	**.3833**	**.6617**	**.7616**	**.7705**	**.9477**	—	—

odds of advancement for boys range from .3833 to .7705 times the odds
for girls, until the final stage (category 4 versus 5), where the likelihood
of advancing for both genders is about the same (OR = .9477).

As mentioned earlier, the process of fitting a CR model to these data
involves restructuring the data set so that each child has as many lines as his
or her outcome score allows (Allison, 1999; Bender & Benner, 2000; Clogg
& Shihadeh, 1994). Basically, this restructured data set contains five concatenated but different data sets representing outcomes for the six proficiency levels in terms of whether or not a child is beyond each category. The
first data set contains all observations, and children who have a proficiency
score beyond 0 are given a value of 1 on a new variable called "beyond"; otherwise, they are given a value of 0 on "beyond." The second data set drops
any child who did not attain at least level 1, and the process is repeated. That
is, children who have a proficiency score beyond 1 receive a score of 1 on
"beyond," otherwise a 0. For the next data set, children in proficiency level 1
are dropped (along with the children who were dropped earlier), and children
with proficiency beyond 2 are given a score of 1 on "beyond," else a 0. The
final stage of the process contains only children who reached at least level 4,
who would then receive a 1 on "beyond" if they continue on to mastery of

level 5, otherwise a 0. In this example, children who stopped out (stopped being tested) at proficiency category 3 would contribute four lines of information to the concatenated data set, with "beyond" scores of 1, 1, 1, and 0 representing their progress in categories 0 through 3, respectively. Syntax C1 in the appendix shows how to create this restructured data set in SAS; an equivalent process can be followed in SPSS. Overall, the total sample size in the restructured data set will correspond to the number of persons included at each step. For the ECLS-K example, this becomes $n = 1 \times f(0) + 2 \times f(1) + 3 \times f(2) + 4 \times f(3) + 5 \times (f(4) + f(5)) = 13,053$.

The variable "beyond" is now the new outcome variable of interest. We are interested in modeling P(beyond) = 1, controlling for stage (or data set or conditional logit comparison), which can be done in SAS PROC LOGIS-TIC using the descending option and the logit link (syntax C2). In the restructuring syntax, the term "crcp" (an acronym for continuation ratio cutpoints) indicates which logit comparison or data set or stage (category) is being referred to. These variables were then dummy coded for the analysis (dumcr0 to dumcr3) using the final comparison as the referent. The results for this binary logistic model with *gender* as the only predictor are summarized in Table 5.2, which also includes the results for the five separate *gender*-only binary logistic regressions that correspond to each of the nested continuation ratio splits presented earlier in Table 4.1. Because this model is inherently different from the CO model presented in Chapter 4, slopes should not be compared between the CO and CR logit-link analyses. The CR and CO logit-link models predict very different sets of probabilities.

In interpreting the results of the CR analysis, the first question that should be addressed is whether or not the model fits. There are two components to this: (1) overall model fit, which can be assessed by comparing the likelihood of the fitted model with the likelihood of the null, or intercept-only, model; and (2) investigating the assumption of parallel odds, or equal slopes in the logit model across the different response-level comparisons being conducted.

As seen in Table 5.2, the fitted model reproduces the data better than the null model, $\chi^2_5 = 4,070.84$, $p < .0001$. This is true as well for each of the separate underlying conditional logit models, with the exception of the last comparison, between children in categories 4 versus 5. Thus, it would be reasonable to investigate whether the parsimony of the global logistic CR model represents the data well enough relative to a simultaneously fitting of the separate models. This investigation would also provide an overall test of the parallel odds assumption.

Similar to the partial proportional odds model, interaction terms can be created between the independent variable of *gender* and each of the dummy-coded variables that represent the continuation ratio cutpoints. If

TABLE 5.2

CR Model (Logit Link) Using Restructured Data Set, $N = 13{,}053$; and
Logistic Regression Results for Each of the Five Conditional Binary
Logistic Models (P(Beyond Category j|Response in at Least Category j))

	CR	0 vs. above	1 vs. above	2 vs. above	3 vs. above	4 vs. above
Intercept	−.3763**	4.478**	2.606**	1.545**	−.330**	−.474**
dumcr0	4.4248**					
dumcr1	2.9113**					
dumcr2	1.9283**					
dumcr3	.0578					
gender	−.2865**	−.956**	−.412**	−.272**	−.261**	−.054
(OR)	**(.751)**	**(.384)**	**(.662)**	**(.762)**	**(.770)**	**(.948)**
Model fit						
−2LL (model)	10,021.534	643.899	1,896.434	2,985.667	3,233.103	1,251.899
χ^2 $(df)^a$	4,070.84^b (5)	13.568 (1)	10.683 (1)	8.830 (1)	9.740 (1)	.157 (1)
	$p < .0001$	$p < .001$	$p = .001$	$p = .003$	$p = .002$	$p = .692$

a. Likelihood ratio chi-square.
b. This test is based on $n = 13{,}053$ observations.
**$p < .01$.

the assumption of equal slopes holds, then it would be expected that the
interaction terms are not necessary to improve the fit of the model. If there
is an interaction between the IV and the cutpoints, this suggests that the
effect of the IV is not homogeneous across the cutpoints of the analysis. In
general, interactions between explanatory variables and the indicator codes
for the cutpoints can be used to create unconstrained CR models where
effects for all explanatory variables are allowed to vary across cutpoints, or
partial CR models where the assumption of parallelism is relaxed for just a
subset of the explanatory variables. This approach mirrors the development
of the non- and partial-proportional odds models presented in Chapter 4.

Four interaction terms were added to the six-parameter additive model.
The resulting $-2LL_{int}$ for the interaction model is 10,011.002 (analysis not
shown), and for the equal slopes model is $-2LL_{no-int} = 10{,}021.534$. Their
difference is 10.532, on four degrees of freedom (number of interaction
terms added to the model). This difference exceeds the critical $\chi^2_{4,\ .05} =$
9.49, but not at $\chi^2_{4,\ .01} = 13.28$. Given the large sample size, we might rea-
sonably assume that the slopes for the interaction terms as a set are not statistically different from zero. However, the slope estimates and ORs for the
separate binary logistic regressions provide useful information regarding
possible differential effects of *gender* across the response levels that is not
apparent through the global and more parsimonious CR (non-interaction)
method. Perhaps additional explanatory variables are needed, or the assumption of parallel odds is inappropriate for the data. Despite the marginal

statistical significance of the parallel odds assumption at $\alpha = .05$, for pedagogical purposes we will continue to explore the statistics and results associated with the CR model under the assumption of equal slopes.

Note that the sum of the model deviances ($-2LL(model)$) for the separate binary logistic regressions in Table 5.2 is equal to the model deviance for the interaction CR analysis described above ($\Sigma[-2LL(model)] = 10,011.002$). The nested dichotomies are independent (Fox, 1997), and thus, the "sum of the separate G^2 [deviance] statistics is an overall goodness-of-fit statistic pertaining to the simultaneous fitting of the models" (Agresti, 1996, p. 219).

To investigate the assumption of parallel odds further, the slopes and ORs from the separate binary logistic regressions can be reviewed and compared informally with the CR results. Alternatively, a process similar to that of summing the multiple model deviances can be conducted for each variable in the model, by summing the Wald test statistics across the series of CR splits (Fox, 1997). Regardless of which approach is favored, it is always wise to look at the logistic regression results for the separate splits; that is the approach taken here.

Returning to the estimates in Table 5.2, the effect for *gender* in the logistic CR model is $-.2865$ ($p < .01$), with a corresponding OR = $\exp(-.2865)$ = .751. This OR summarizes the general trend seen earlier, in the original data (Table 5.1): Boys are less likely to advance beyond a given mastery level relative to girls. To calculate the estimated odds ratios for the conditional comparisons, the CR model can be used to calculate the logits. With the referent as the final comparison in the dummy-coding scheme employed, the intercept is used to find the logit for being beyond proficiency level 4, that is, for $(Y > 4|Y \geq 4)$: $logit_{cr4} = -.3763 + (-.2865 \times gender)$. For boys, $logit_{cr4} = -.6628$; for girls, $logit_{cr4} = -.3763$. From these values, estimated conditional probabilities are found. For boys, $\hat{\delta}_4 = [\exp(-.6628)/(1 + \exp(-.6628)] = .3401$; similarly, $\hat{\delta}_4$ for girls is .4070. Finally, the odds for boys and girls can be determined and used to calculate the estimated OR_4, which is .7509. Predictions for all comparisons are summarized in Table 5.3. Using the CR model, the odds ratios across all continuation ratio cutpoints are equivalent and approximately .75. The CR model constrains these odds to be equal across all sequential conditional category comparisons.

Comparing the estimated ORs from the CR model to the actual ORs for *gender*, both in Table 5.3, we see there is more similarity toward the middle of the ordinal proficiency scale than there is at either end. Although the common odds ratio is in the right direction and the overall model can be interpreted to indicate that boys are less likely than girls to be beyond any given category, this lack of homogeneity deserves some further attention in order to make a wise decision regarding balance between model parsimony and clarification of evident variable effects.

TABLE 5.3

Observed Proportions (δ_j) for $P(Y > j | Y \geq j)$, Predictions, and Observed and Estimated ORs for *Gender* Model, CR Analysis With Logit Link

	Category					
	0	*1*	*2*	*3*	*4*	*5*
Males						
δ_j	.9713	.8997	.7811	.3564	.3710	
logits	3.762	2.2485	1.2655	−.6050	−.6628	—
$\hat{\delta}_j$	.9773	.9045	.7798	.3532	.3401	—
$(1 - \hat{\delta}_j)$	(.0227)	(.0955)	(.2202)	(.6468)	(.6599)	
Females						
δ_j	.9888	.9313	.8241	.4182	.3836	
logits	4.0485	2.535	1.552	−.3185	−.3763	—
$\hat{\delta}_j$	.9829	.9266	.8252	.4211	.4070	—
$(1 - \hat{\delta}_j)$	(.0171)	(.0734)	(.1748)	(.5789)	(.5930)	
OR (obs.)	.3833	.6617	.7616	.7705	.9477	—
OR (est.)	.7490	.7502	.7501	.7508	.7509	

Reviewing the binary logistic regression models formed from the conditional data sets in Table 5.2, we see additional evidence of heterogeneity in the slope estimates for *gender* across the separate splits, in terms of both magnitude and statistical significance. For the binary models, the effects of *gender* on the log-odds range from −.054 to −.956, with an average slope of −.391. This average slope corresponds to an OR of .676. For the last binary logit comparison ($Y > 4 | Y \geq 4$), the effect of *gender* is not statistically significant, and its OR is close to 1.0. Although the CR model gives a parsimonious view of the effect of *gender* across all the separate logit comparisons, and on average it seems to correspond with the separate fits, there is some justified apprehension in using the CR model fitted here. In some research situations, presenting and discussing the results for the separate comparisons may be a more reasonable and informative option than focusing solely on the more global results of the CR model.

Recall that the purpose of the CR model is to investigate the probabilities of being beyond a given proficiency level, given a response at or beyond that proficiency level. The predictions from the model provided in Table 5.3 should reasonably replicate the observed conditional probabilities associated with each continuation ratio, $P(Y > j | Y \geq j)$. Based on the results of the CR analysis, which constrains the *gender* effect to be equivalent across the continuation ratio cutpoints, the model's predictions seem to be quite close to the observed conditional probabilities for both boys and girls. For future reference, the estimated complementary probabilities are provided in Table 5.3 as well. These complementary probabilities are $P(Y = j | Y \geq j)$, which from our earlier discussion represent estimates of the hazard, or failure rate, that is, the probability of *not* advancing beyond proficiency category j.

Somers' D for these data was .691, indicating good correspondence between observed and predicted probabilities for being beyond a given category, although this rank-order correlation coefficient is for the restructured binary-outcome data and not the original ordinal responses. The likelihood ratio $R^2_L = .289$, indicating moderate reduction in deviance for the CR model, relative to the null or intercept-only model; again, this coefficient is for the restructured binary-outcome data set.

To investigate predictive efficiency via τ_p and λ_p, the classification table can be constructed using estimated conditional probabilities. SAS will save the $P(\text{beyond} = 1)$ for each of the $N = 13{,}053$ cases in the restructured data set. Aggregating this data set back to the original size sample, however, can be problematic, because only people who were included in each conditional comparison will have predictions for that split. Therefore, a convenient way to create the classification table is to enter the model estimates into a statistical program and use these estimates on the original data set ($N = 3{,}365$) to compute the logits based on *gender*. The logits can then be transformed to the conditional probabilities, $\delta_j = \exp(\text{logit}_j)/(1 + \exp(\text{logit}_j))$, so that each child has an estimate for each conditional comparison, $P(Y > \text{cat. } j | Y \geq \text{cat. } j)$. This process yields the same estimates as those provided in Table 5.3.

The category probabilities can then be found using the following relationship (Läärä & Matthews, 1985):

$$(1 - \delta_j(\underline{x})) = \frac{\pi_j(\underline{x})}{1 - \gamma_{j-1}(\underline{x})},$$

where $\delta_j(\underline{x}) = P(Y > \text{cat. } j | Y \geq \text{cat. } j, \underline{x})$, $\pi_j(\underline{x}) = P(Y = \text{cat. } j | \underline{x})$, and $\gamma_j(\underline{x}) = P(Y \leq \text{cat. } j | \underline{x}) = \pi_0(\underline{x}) + \pi_1(\underline{x}) + \ldots \pi_j(\underline{x})$. Rearranging terms to solve for the category probabilities, $\pi_j(\underline{x})$, we have $\pi_j(\underline{x}) = (1 - \delta_j(\underline{x})) \times (1 - \gamma_{j-1}(\underline{x}))$. This results in six category probabilities, one for each level of the response. Individual category membership is assigned to the category with the greatest probability for that child. The syntax for this process is provided in the appendix as syntax C8.

For the *gender*-only model, the logistic CR model predicts all children into category 3. Similar to the CO model in Chapter 4, $\tau_p = .23$ and $\lambda_p = 0$. Although the pattern of estimated probabilities may be informative, the one-variable model does not seem to be very useful in terms of accuracy of proficiency classifications. Nonetheless, the approach outlined here could easily be followed for CR analysis of more complex models as well as other ordinal data sets.

EXAMPLE 5.2: Continuation Ratio
Model With Complementary Log-Log Link

As a result of its straightforward correspondence with the underlying binary logistic regression models, the logit-link function is often used in research studies where continuation ratio models are desired. An alternative link function is the complementary log-log (clog-log) link, which provides an interpretation of the results in terms of a hazard ratio rather than an odds ratio. Example syntax for a CR analysis using the restructured data set with the clog-log link is contained in Appendix C3, with two changes from the previous logit-link analysis. First, the link requested was clog-log. Second, the ascending approach rather than the descending approach was used, in order to correspond to an interpretation of (transformed) model estimates as predicted hazards. That is, for the restructured data set, we wish to predict P(beyond $= 0$) rather than P(beyond $= 1$).

Recall that the conditional probability, $P(Y_i = \text{cat. } j | Y_i \geq \text{cat. } j)$, provides an estimate of the hazard. Using the ascending option with the clog-log link, this estimated probability is the *complement* of that predicted by the logit-link model; that is, the logit model estimated the conditional probability of being *beyond* category j, or $P(Y_i > \text{cat. } j | Y_i \geq \text{cat. } j)$, whereas the clog-log model as constructed here estimates the conditional probability of *stopping out* in category j, $P(Y_i = \text{cat. } j | Y_i \geq \text{cat. } j)$. This correspondence allows the estimated continuation ratios and/or their complements for the two link functions to be directly compared. Without the ascending option, the fitted clog-log model would be estimating an entirely different set of conditional probabilities, namely, $P(Y_i < \text{cat. } j | Y_i \leq \text{cat. } j)$. Caution must be taken to ensure that the appropriate event of interest (here, $Y = \text{cat. } j | Y \geq \text{cat. } j$) as well as its desired complement (here, $Y > \text{cat. } j | Y \geq \text{cat. } j$) matches the predictions of interest to the researcher. The first two columns of Table 5.4 provide the results of this analysis using the Logistic Regression procedure in SAS.

The clog-log link function transforms the observed probabilities quite differently than does the method used with the logit link. The values formed via the clog-log link function are not the logs of the odds, but the logs of the hazards, thus representing the proportional hazards model. Similar to the logit link of the previous section, discussing Example 5.1, the response variable is transformed based on the conditional probabilities: $p = P(Y_i = \text{cat. } j | Y_i \geq \text{cat. } j)$. However, where the logit was defined as the log of the odds, the clog-log is defined as the log of the negative log of the

TABLE 5.4

Parameter Estimates for CR Models With Clog-Log Link on
Restructured Data Set, N = 13,053; and on Original Data Set, N = 3,365

	Restructured		Original
Intercept	−.1166*	Intercept 0	−4.0091**
dumcr0	−3.8924**	Intercept 1	−2.3257**
dumcr1	−2.4146**	Intercept 2	−1.2173**
dumcr2	−1.5013**	Intercept 3	.1444**
dumcr3	−.0350	Intercept 4	.7155**
gender	**.1976**	*gender*	**.1976**
Model fit			
−2LL (model)	10,026.201		10,026.201
−2LL (null)	14,092.374		10,053.980
χ^2 (*df*)	4,066.173** (5)		27.7511** (1)

*p < .05; **p < .01.

complementary probability: clog-log = log(–log(1 – p)). To use the clog-log predictions to return the data to conditional probabilities, the inverse of this process is used: *p-hat* = 1 – exp(–exp(clog-log)). As with the proportional odds model, a restrictive assumption is placed on the data: proportional hazards. This assumption, also referred to as the parallel or equal slopes assumption, requires the hazards (where hazard = exp(clog-log)) to maintain homogeneous proportionality across all levels of the response variable. A demonstration of this assumption follows.

Based on syntax C3 in the appendix, we see from the summary of results in Table 5.4 that the model fits better than the null, χ^2_5 = 4,066.173, p < .0001. In this analysis, the effect of *gender* on the clog-logs is +.1976, which is statistically different from zero (p < .01). Singer and Willett (2003) point out that regardless of choice of link function, we exponentiate the estimates from the model for interpretation purposes: "Whereas an antilogged coefficient from a model with a logit link is an odds ratio, an antilogged coefficient from a model with a clog-log link is a hazard ratio" (p. 424). Exponentiating the *gender* effect for our current model, we find the hazards ratio, HR = exp(.1976) = 1.218. Across all response levels for the proficiency categories 0 through 5, the hazard for boys of being at a particular level *j* rather than beyond, relative to girls, is assumed constant at 1.28. To understand what this means for our data, the model estimates and predicted probabilities for the clog-log model are provided in Table 5.5a. The notation $h\hat{\delta}_j$ is used to indicate predicted conditional probabilities based on the clog-log link model to distinguish between the continuation ratios estimated through the logit-link analysis.

Probability predictions for boys versus girls can best be understood in terms of their corresponding hazards, as determined through the fitted

TABLE 5.5a

Observed Proportions (δ_j) for $P(Y > j | Y \geq j)$, Predictions, Estimated Hazards and Complements, and Estimated HRs for *Gender* Models, CR Analyses With Clog-Log Link (Using Restructured Data Set)

	Category					
	0	*1*	*2*	*3*	*4*	*5*
Males						
$\delta_{j\,(obs)}$	.9713	.8997	.7811	.3564	.3710	—
clog-log	−3.8114	−2.3336	−1.4203	.046	.081	
$h\hat{\delta}_j$	.0219	.0924	.2147	.6490	.6619	
$1 - h\hat{\delta}_j$	.9781	.9076	.7853	.3510	.3381	
Females						
$\delta_{j\,(obs)}$	.9888	.9313	.8241	.4182	.3836	
clog-log	−4.009	−2.5312	−1.6179	−.1516	−.1166	—
$h\hat{\delta}_j$	.0180	.0765	.1780	.5766	.5893	—
$1 - h\hat{\delta}_j$	.9820	.9235	.8220	.4234	.4107	
HR[a] (est.)	1.218	1.218	1.218	1.218	1.218	—

NOTE: $h\hat{\delta}_j = p\text{-}hat = P(Y = \text{cat. } j | Y \geq \text{cat. } j)$.
a. Hazard = exp(clog-log); HR = (hazard(boys))/(hazard(girls)).

model. With the ascending option in place, the predictions are for $h\hat{\delta}_j = P(Y = j | Y \geq j)$; this is complementary to the predictions found in the logit-link CR analysis. Complementary probabilities derived from the clog-log model, $1 - h\hat{\delta}_j = P(Y > j | Y \geq j)$, are also presented in Table 5.5a.

Recall that in these models, boys have a coded value of *gender* = 1, whereas girls have a coded value of *gender* = 0; the dummy coding used for the cutpoints implies that the intercept corresponds to the final comparison of $Y = 4$ to $Y = 5$. To find the clog-log estimates for boys for the first continuation ratio (which compares $Y = 0$ to $Y \geq 0$), we find that (using Table 5.4) clog-log$_{boys,\,0}$ = −.1166 + (−3.8924) × dumcr0 + (.1976) × *gender* = −3.8114. For girls, the model estimate corresponds to clog-log$_{girls,\,0}$ = −.1166 + (−3.8924) × dumcr0 = −4.009. Exponentiating each clog-log and taking the ratio of boys to girls, we have the hazards ratio, HR = exp(−3.8114)/ exp(−4.009) = 1.218. It is this ratio that the model constrains to be constant across all continuation ratio comparisons. The HRs calculated based on the clog-log estimates in Table 5.5a for each continuation ratio comparison are all, within rounding error, equal to 1.218. The hazard for boys of *not* advancing is assumed to be greater than that for girls and constant across the conditional continuation ratio cutpoints. This implies that boys are more likely than girls *not* to attain the higher reading

TABLE 5.5b

Observed Proportions (δ_j) for $P(Y > j | Y \geq j)$, Predictions, Estimated
Probabilities and Complements, and Estimated HRs for *Gender* Models,
CR Analyses With Clog-Log Link (Using Original Data Set)

	Category					
	0	*1*	*2*	*3*	*4*	*5*
Males						
δ_j	.9713	.8997	.7811	.3564	.3710	
clog-log	−3.812	−2.122	−1.020	.3420	.9131	—
$c\hat{\delta}_j$	.0219	.1123	.3028	.7553	.9173	—
$1 - c\hat{\delta}_j$	.9781	.8877	.6972	.2447	.0827	
Females						
δ_j	.9888	.9313	.8241	.4182	.3836	
clog-log	−4.009	−2.323	−1.217	.1444	.7155	—
$c\hat{\delta}_j$	.0180	.0931	.2562	.6850	.8707	—
$1 - c\hat{\delta}_j$	.9820	.9069	.7438	.3150	.1293	
HR[a] (est.)	1.218	1.218	1.218	1.218	1.218	—

NOTE: $c\hat{\delta}_j$ = cumulative probabilities
a. Hazard = exp(clog-log); HR = (hazard(boys))/(hazard(girls)).

proficiency levels, which is consistent with the results of the logistic CR model.

To investigate the assumption of equal slopes, four interaction terms representing the interaction between *gender* and each split were added to the model. The $-2LL_{int}$ = 10,011.002 (analysis not shown), and when compared to the $-2LL_{non-int}$ = 10,026.201, the difference is χ^2_4 = 15.20, which exceeds $\chi^2_{4, .005}$ = 14.86. This suggests that the hazards are *not* parallel across outcome categories for the single explanatory variable of *gender*. For demonstration purposes, however, we will continue to explore the interpretation of parameter estimates and predicted probabilities for the parallel slopes model.

The estimated conditional probabilities, notated by $h\hat{\delta}_j$, are found by taking the inverse of the link function for the predicted clog-logs in the *gender* model. That is, *p-hat* = $h\hat{\delta}_j$ = 1 − exp(−exp(clog-log)). We can compare the predictions for the complements, $1 - h\hat{\delta}_j$, to the observed continuation ratios in the first row of Table 5.5a, and their close correspondence to the actual data is clear.

Are the predictions based on the clog-log link more accurate than those obtained through the logit link? For the clog-log link, R^2_L = .289, and Somers' D = .691, which are the same (within rounding) for the logit-link model. The two link functions seem to be performing equally well. In terms of predictive efficiency, we see the same pattern of predicted probabilities under both link functions; with *gender* as the only predictor in this simple model, the estimated proficiency level for both boys and girls would be category 3; as a result, $\tau_p = .23$ and $\lambda_p = 0$. The classification table was derived using a process similar to that followed in the logistic CR analysis and solving for *p-hat* from the predicted clog-logs, rather than logits. Further, the complementary probabilities do not need to be solved for when creating the classification table (if modifying the syntax in Appendix C8), because the predicted probabilities for the ascending clog-log model are already $h\delta_j = P(Y = \text{cat. } j | Y \geq \text{cat. } j)$. Based on the predictive efficiency statistics, no preference is obvious for either the logit or the clog-log link. The logit model, however, did meet the assumption of equal slopes more strongly than did the clog-log model.

Choice of Link and Equivalence of Two Clog-Log Models

In general, fit statistics for the CR model under either the logit or clog-log link function should be comparable, as we have seen here. The choice between link functions comes down to a matter of preference for the advantages of either approach, and to a conceptual understanding of how the data were generated. Advantages of the logit link include its simplicity of interpretation in terms of odds and odds ratios. Advantages of the clog-log link include its interpretation in terms of hazards and hazards ratios, and its direct connection to the proportional hazards model. For the analyses presented here, "time" is not a structural component of how the data were generated, so a stronger argument could be made in favor of the logit approach. However, with either link function, stage-specific interactions can be directly included and tested in the models, so investigation of the equal slopes assumption can easily be assessed.

Computationally, however, restructuring a large data set to fit the continuation ratio model can begin to get cumbersome, particularly as the number of response levels increases. With the clog-log link, the original data set can be used and the proportional odds model of the previous chapter applied. As shown by Läärä and Matthews (1985), the results of this approach are directly comparable to the continuation ratio model obtained through the clog-log link applied to the restructured data set. Both models yield the same variable effects, which can be used to provide a direct interpretation of the patterns in the data in terms of hazards ratios. Further, with this approach, a test of the equal slopes assumption is provided in either SAS or SPSS. However, whereas the CR model provides estimates of conditional probabilities when the restructured data set is used, the *cumulative* CR model provides estimates of *cumulative* probabilities. Syntax C4 in the appendix shows how to fit this model in SAS using the ascending option; thus, the model is predicting $P(Y \leq \text{cat. } j)$. The equivalent SPSS syntax is shown in Syntax C5. SAS results using the original data set for the single explanatory variable of *gender* are shown in the second half of Table 5.4.

Note first that the effect of *gender*, $b = .1976$ ($p < .01$), is equivalent between the two clog-log link models. That is, in terms of effects of explanatory variables, using the clog-log link on the restructured data set for a binary outcome is equivalent to the use of the clog-log link in a cumulative odds model. Parameter estimates from either approach are interpreted in terms of hazards. As we saw earlier, the hazard for boys of *not* achieving beyond a given proficiency level is $\exp(.1976) = 1.28$ times the hazard for girls. The intercept values between the two clog-log link models, however, are not equivalent, and in general this is due to the very different structures of the two models. There is no expectation that the intercepts would be comparable, because one model predicts conditional probabilities (clog-log link on the restructured data) and the other predicts cumulative probabilities (clog-log link on the original ordinal data). The predictions in terms of probabilities are not equivalent.

Predictions from the clog-log link on the restructured data were provided in Table 5.5a; predictions from the cumulative CR model where the clog-log link was applied to the original data set are shown in Table 5.5b. Recall that the predicted probabilities are found by $p\text{-hat} = 1 - \exp(-\exp(\text{clog-log}))$. Here, the notation $c\hat{\delta}_j$ is used to distinguish these predicted probabilities from those in the previous analysis. The predictions for the cumulative CR model can be compared back to the actual cumulative probabilities (cp) in Table 4.2. In terms of cumulative probabilities, the model seems to reflect the actual data well. Evidence of fit, however, for this one-variable model is small. Somers' D for this analysis is .079, and $R^2_L = .003$. For the pseudo R^2's, we find $R^2_{CS} = .008$ and $R^2_N = .009$. Further, $\tau_p = .23$ and $\lambda_p = 0$, as the *gender*-only cumulative model predicts all children into category 3 regardless of link function.

The score test for the equal slopes assumption yields a $\chi^2_4 = 14.95$, with $p = .0048$, suggesting that the parameter estimates are not equivalent across categories. Brant (1990) identifies several problems with the score test regardless of link function. Large samples tend to yield small p values, so conclusions based on the score test may be flawed; that is, decisions to reject the assumption of proportional odds may not coincide with substantively meaningful differences across the category comparisons for any or all of the explanatory variables. Additionally, the score test provides only a global assessment of lack of fit to the assumption of parallel slopes, with no information about the nature of the departure from the assumption. As was emphasized in Chapter 4, Brant's recommendation is to investigate the underlying binary models that accompany the approach to the ordinal analysis, in order to "evaluate the aptness of the model while gaining added insight into the complexities of the data" (1990, p. 1176). Although for space considerations the *gender*-only binary models under the clog-log link function are not examined, it would be quite reasonable to do so, in order to augment the information obtained from the global score test.

Choice of Approach for Continuation Ratio Models

As we saw in Chapter 4, the logit link was used to fit the proportional odds model when the outcome variable was ordinal. The proportional odds model with the logit link is probably the most common choice among competing models for research in the social sciences, but for ordinal outcomes, there are compelling reasons to consider fitting continuation ratio models. As we have seen here, there are several different ways that the CR model can be developed. Substantively, when the dependent responses represent an ordinal progression through sequential stages, a stronger understanding of factors affecting this progression can be obtained if variable effects on the conditional probabilities (i.e., conditional on reaching a particular stage or not), rather than cumulative probabilities, are estimated. Further, due to its relationship with an underlying proportional hazards model, the clog-log link can provide a parsimonious analysis that explicitly models these variable effects sequentially for each conditional dichotomy.

The logistic CR model is "precisely the proportional 'logit hazard' model considered by [D. R.] Cox (1972) for discrete survival distributions" (C. Cox, 1988, p. 436), providing hazards in discrete time. When the clog-log link is used, the fitted model is the proportional hazards model (Ananth & Kleinbaum, 1997). The choice between the link functions should hinge on the usefulness of results that are obtained under either transformation. Given that many applied researchers in the educational and social sciences are becoming more familiar with logit models, odds, and odds ratios, it is reasonable to expect that the logistic CR approach may be best suited to the study of ordinal outcomes in this domain. The use of the restructured data set to fit these models, regardless of link function, probably is a very wise strategy, in comparison with using the cumulative CR clog-log model. The restructured data set allows for straightforward creation and inclusion of interaction terms, much the same as was done for the PPO example in

Chapter 4. In situations where the assumption of parallel odds doesn't hold for explanatory variables, fitting a partial CR model (Cole & Ananth, 2001) may provide better explanations of effects within the data.

EXAMPLE 5.3: Full-Model Continuation Ratio Analyses for the ECLS-K Data

In this final section, an example of the multivariable logistic CR model is provided for the ECLS-K data. The analysis follows syntax C6 in the appendix, SAS with the descending option. The conditional probabilities of interest are $P(Y > \text{cat. } j | Y \geq \text{cat. } j)$ for the eight-variable model. Table 5.6 provides the results of the analysis; also included in Table 5.6 are the results of the corresponding binary logit analyses for comparison purposes. The final column of Table 5.6 includes the clog-log CR model (hazards) fitted through SPSS PLUM. For illustrative purposes, focus is on the results of the logistic CR analysis.

Overall, boys (*gender*; OR = .688), children with any family risk characteristics (*famrisk*; OR = .808), children who are not read to frequently by their parents or guardians (*noreadbo*; OR = .763), and children who attended only half-day kindergarten (*halfdayK*; OR = .894) are *less* likely to be beyond a given proficiency level. Family SES (*wksesl*; OR = 1.78) and the child's age (*p1ageent*; OR = 1.05) are positively associated with having a greater likelihood of being *beyond* a given proficiency level.

For the most part, these effects are consistent in size and pattern across the corresponding binary models. Some differences are evident, however. The effects of *minority*, as coded here, change dramatically across the binary splits; the global effect of *minority* as estimated through the logistic CR model (OR = .918, n.s.) does not adequately capture the unique effects across all CR comparisons. Additionally, the effect of attending a half-day kindergarten program rather than a full-day program in the logistic CR model (OR = .894, sig.) also does not seem to adequately reflect the potential contribution of length of kindergarten day, as evidenced through the binary CR comparisons.

Despite the irregularities noted, however, the model fit statistic for the logistic CR analysis indicates that the model does provide a good fit to the data. Measures of association for this analysis are Somers' D = .739, τ_p = .23, and λ_p = 002. Reasonable adjustments to this logistic CR model would include calculation and inclusion of interactions for the *minority* and *halfdayK* explanatory variables, as well as the deletion of the *center* effect (whether or not the child had attended center-based care prior to kindergarten) from the model.

CR-Full-Model (Logit Link) Analyses Using Restructured Data Set, $N = 13{,}053$; Binary CR_j (Logit Link) Analyses for $P(Y > \text{cat. } j | Y \geq \text{cat. } j)$; and SPSS Clog-Log PLUM Analysis

	Logistic CR b (se(b)) OR	CR_0 b (se(b)) OR	CR_1 b (se(b)) OR	CR_2 b (se(b)) OR	CR_3 b (se(b)) OR	CR_4 b (se(b)) OR	Clog-Log CR b (se(b)) HR
Int1[a]	-3.80 (.45)**	3.53 (2.11)	-.85 (1.08)	-1.60 (.80)*	-3.51 (.73)**	-3.71 (1.21)**	$\theta_0 = -1.308\ (.339)$**
Int2 (dumer0)	4.89 (.15)**						$\theta_1 = .391\ (.321)$
Int3 (dumer1)	3.33 (.10)**						$\theta_2 = 1.527\ (.319)$**
Int4 (dumer2)	2.26 (.09)**						$\theta_3 = 2.960\ (.320)$**
Int5 (dumer3)	0.20 (.08)*						$\theta_4 = 3.588\ (.322)$**
gender	-.374 (.052) .688**	-1.039 (.283) .354**	-.489 (.131) .613*	-.363 (.095) .695*	-.338 (.087) .713*	-.119 (.141) .888	.242 (.038) 1.274**
famrisk	-.2137 (.062) .808**	-.145 (.295) .865	-.291 (.146) .748*	-.169 (.108) .844	-.259 (.106) .772*	-.021 (.180) .979	.150 (.045) 1.162**
center	.089 (.062) 1.093	.034 (.284) .966	-.086 (.149) .917	.188 (.108) 1.207	.072 (.108) 1.075	.200 (.187) 1.221	-.069 (.045) .933
noreadbo	-.271 (.072) .763**	-.654 (.272) .520**	-.283 (.154) .754	-.200 (.123) .819	-.172 (.133) .842	-.335 (.245) .715	.185 (.052) 1.203**
minority	-.085 (.058) .918	-.228 (.288) .796	-.461 (.142) .631*	-.324 (.103) .723*	.250 (.097) 1.284*	.158 (.156) 1.171	.030 (.043) 1.03**
halfdayk	-.112 (.053) .894*	-.074 (.261) .928	.026 (.133) 1.027	-.136 (.097) .873	-.254 (.087) .776*	.130 (.141) 1.139	.079 (.039)* 1.08*
wksesl	.575 (.039) 1.777**	1.005 (.168) 2.71**	.632 (.100) 1.865*	.582 (.076) 1.790*	.451 (.063) 1.570*	.600 (.102) *1.823	.402 (.029) 1.495
plqgeent	.049 (.007) 1.05**	.024 (.032) 1.025	.061 (.016) 1.062*	.050 (.012) 1.051*	.048 (.011) 1.049*	.041 (.018) 1.042*	.033 (.005) 1.034
Model $\chi^2(df)$	4548.76** (12)	82.11** (8)	146.74** (8)	180.62** (8)	123.88** (8)	56.58** (8)	449.99** (8)
Parallel slopes $\chi^2(df)$							134.431 (32)**
H-L $\chi^2(df)$	7.796 (8)	7.796 (8)	7.495 (8)	13.869 (8)	6.118 (8)	9.392 (7)	
p	.454 (n.s.)	.454 (n.s.)	.484 (n.s.)	.085 (n.s.)	.634 (n.s.)	.310 (n.s.)	

NOTE: For logit-link analysis, parameter estimates are for category = 1 for categorical variables; category = 0 for SPSS PLUM analysis.
a. For logistic CR, corresponds to last comparison: category 4 versus above (category 5) through dummy coding.
*p < .05; **p < .01.

6. THE ADJACENT CATEGORIES MODEL

Overview of the Adjacent Categories Model

A third option for the analysis of ordinal response variables (along with CO and CR models) involves simultaneous estimates of the effects of explanatory variables in pairs of adjacent categories. Adjacent category (AC) models are a specific form of generalized logit models for multinomial outcomes (Clogg & Shihadeh, 1994; Goodman, 1983; Hosmer & Lemeshow, 2000). In the multinomial approach, comparisons are made between each response outcome and a base category, generally taken as the last response category. The multinomial model is unconstrained, in that effects of explanatory variables are allowed to vary for each specific comparison. In AC models, these effects are constrained to be constant or homogeneous for comparisons of *adjacent* categories, mirroring the assumptions of proportionality and parallelism that were described previously for the CO and CR models. Goodman (1979) refers to this assumption as "uniform association."

SAS estimates the AC model through PROC CATMOD, although the analysis is not optimal for models that contain continuous explanatory variables. PROC CATMOD estimates the model through weighted least squares, which requires that the data be grouped as in a contingency table (Allison, 1999; SAS, 1999). Continuous variables can be categorized for inclusion in the AC model, a strategy used by Clogg and Shihadeh (1994), but this approach may have implications for model fit if the effects of the continuous variables are not linear across the response levels. Further, the sample sizes within each profile of individuals in the sample sharing similar values for the explanatory variables need to be large enough for reliable estimation across the AC comparisons (Stokes et al., 2000). Despite the shortcomings of current software designed to fit AC models, this approach does offer a reasonable alternative to either the CO or the CR method for research situations in which comparisons across adjacent categories makes strong theoretical sense.

In AC models, the logit transformation compares $\pi_{i,j}$, the probability of the ith person's response being in category j, to the probability of response in the next successive category, $\pi_{i,j+1}$. The purpose of this approach is to simultaneously determine the odds of response in the *next highest* category for each pair of adjacent categories. A series of logits is constructed, and the analysis corresponds to the comparisons provided in the last section of Table 4.1. We take the log of the two adjacent probabilities to create the logit:

$$Y'_j = \ln\left(\frac{\pi_{i,j+1}}{\pi_{i,j}}\right) = \alpha_j + \beta X_i$$

where J = number of response levels and $j = 1, \ldots J - 1$. In this equation, the probabilities represented by the numerator and the denominator refer to the probabilities for the two adjacent categories being compared. The intercepts in the $J - 1$ logit equations may vary across adjacent category comparisons, but the effects of the explanatory variables are assumed to be constant across these comparisons. The slope effect, β, is homogeneous across all AC comparisons.

The odds ratios for the AC model are referred to as *local odds ratios* because the association they describe is from a localized region in the overall table (Agresti, 1989, 1996). For a single categorical explanatory variable with two levels, 0 and 1, $J - 1$ odds ratio are formed for each specific pair of adjacent categories ($j = 1$ to $J - 1$).

$$OR_{j+1} = \frac{P(Y = j + 1 \mid x = 1)/P(Y_i = j \mid x = 1)}{P(Y = j + 1 \mid x = 0)/P(Y_i = j \mid x = 0)}.$$

The investigation of parallelism for the AC model can proceed much the same way as in the previous analyses, but no formal test for the constraint is available. If the AC model does not fit, a multinomial approach can be formed; or the specific logistic regression splits corresponding to each AC comparison can be reviewed for plausibility of the constraint.

Similar to the previous chapters, in the discussion to follow, the *gender*-only model is fit first in order to describe the methodology, approach, and results of a simple AC analysis. Next, a more complex model is fit, and the results are explained. Syntax for the two models presented here (simple and complex) is included in the appendix, section D.

EXAMPLE 6.1: *Gender*-Only Model

The syntax shown in the appendix, section D1, was used for the simple *gender*-only AC model. In this syntax as well as in the more complex model, the effects of explanatory variables are treated as quantitative and thus are included in the "*direct*" subcommand within PROC CATMOD. Because the coding for *gender* was done externally to SAS (0 = females, 1 = males), this approach allows for ease of interpretation of the effects and keeps the interpretation consistent with those of the previous logit models. (See Stokes et al. [2000] for an alternative but equivalent approach to the treatment of categorical predictors in PROC CATMOD.) The "*response*" statement specifies the adjacent categories model ("*alogit*"), and the syntax asks for the predicted logits and estimated AC probabilities to be written to a file called "*acgender*." Finally, the model specification uses a term on the right side of the equation called "*_response_*." This term imposes the constraint of one common effect of gender across the AC response functions. The estimation process is specified as weighted least squares ("*wls*"), and a table containing the models' predicted logits is requested ("*pred*").

The outcome of proficiency in early reading has six possible responses (0, 1, 2, 3, 4, 5); thus, there are $6 - 1 = 5$ response functions representing the adjacent category comparisons. Figure 6.1 provides a subset of the major results of the statistical analysis through PROC CATMOD. First, the "Population Profiles" report the sample sizes for each unique covariate pattern. With *gender* as the only explanatory variable in this model, the sample sizes here refer to the sample size for each of the *gender* groups, referred to as "*samples*." As the number of explanatory variables increases, this table can be useful in identifying sparse samples for particular covariate patterns.

The "Analysis of Variance" section provides a test for the effect of *gender* across the $J - 1 = 5$ AC response functions. According to this analysis, the effect of *gender* is statistically significant, $\chi^2_1 = 38.38$, $p < .0001$. The residual chi-square test indicates that the model fits, $\chi^2_4 = 2.96$, $p = .5647$. This chi-square test-statistic is a goodness-of-fit test similar to the Pearson chi-square test comparing a fitted model to a perfect or saturated model.

The weighted least squares estimates are shown in the next section of the printout. There are five terms that are used collectively to determine the intercept for each of the response functions, along with one term that represents the effect of *gender* across all the AC comparisons. The intercept for each successive response function is found by adding the intercept term to the corresponding _response_ value. Table 6.1 illustrates this process for the intercepts of the $J - 1 = 5$ response functions. Based on the results shown in Table 6.1, the five response models for this simple analysis are

$$\hat{Y}'(1, 0) = 1.5725 + (-.1928) \times \textit{gender}$$

$$\hat{Y}'(2, 1) = .8688 + (-.1928) \times \textit{gender}$$

$$\hat{Y}'(3, 2) = 1.0146 + (-.1928) \times \textit{gender}$$

$$\hat{Y}'(4, 3) = -.8347 + (-.1928) \times \textit{gender}$$

$$\hat{Y}'(5, 4) = -.4147 + (-.1928) \times \textit{gender}$$

```
                    Population Profiles

          Sample     GENDER     Sample Size
          ƒƒƒƒƒƒƒƒƒƒƒƒƒƒƒƒƒƒƒƒƒƒƒƒƒƒƒƒƒƒƒƒ
            1          0           1692
            2          1           1673


                 Analysis of Variance

       Source        DF    Chi-Square   Pr > ChiSq
       ƒƒƒƒƒƒƒƒƒƒƒƒƒƒƒƒƒƒƒƒƒƒƒƒƒƒƒƒƒƒƒƒƒƒƒƒƒƒƒƒƒƒ
       Intercept      1      176.21       <.0001
       _RESPONSE_     4     1550.56       <.0001
       GENDER         1       38.38       <.0001

       Residual       4        2.96       0.5647


         Analysis of Weighted Least Squares Estimates

                                Standard   Chi-
       Parameter        Estimate   Error   Square   Pr > ChiSq
       ƒƒƒƒƒƒƒƒƒƒƒƒƒƒƒƒƒƒƒƒƒƒƒƒƒƒƒƒƒƒƒƒƒƒƒƒƒƒƒƒƒƒƒƒƒƒƒƒƒƒƒƒƒ
       Intercept         0.4323   0.0326   176.21     <.0001
       _RESPONSE_    1   1.0952   0.1158    89.48     <.0001
                     2   0.4365   0.0774    31.81     <.0001
                     3   0.5823   0.0554   110.40     <.0001
                     4  -1.2670   0.0558   515.67     <.0001
       GENDER          -0.1928   0.0311    38.38     <.0001


              Predicted Values for Response Functions

               ------Observed------    ------Predicted-----

        Function          Standard           Standard
GENDER  Number  Function   Error    Function   Error    Residual
ƒƒƒƒƒƒƒƒƒƒƒƒƒƒƒƒƒƒƒƒƒƒƒƒƒƒƒƒƒƒƒƒƒƒƒƒƒƒƒƒƒƒƒƒƒƒƒƒƒƒƒƒƒƒƒƒƒƒƒƒƒƒƒƒ
0        1     1.800493  0.247643  1.527445  0.139517   0.273048
         2     0.868196  0.111109  0.868796  0.075314   -0.0006
         3     1.002937  0.070628  1.014531  0.051393   -0.01159
         4    -0.81395   0.066029 -0.83477   0.050661    0.020819
         5    -0.47424   0.088744 -0.41475   0.068319   -0.0595

1        1     1.222549  0.16422   1.334673  0.136174   -0.11212
         2     0.674571  0.096229  0.676024  0.073575   -0.00145
         3     0.83155   0.066974  0.82176   0.050663    0.00979
         4    -1.05469   0.072573 -1.02754   0.051874   -0.02716
         5    -0.5279    0.10261  -0.60752   0.069586    0.079621
```

Figure 6.1   PROC CATMOD Results: Simple *Gender* Model

80

TABLE 6.1
Intercepts for the $J - 1 = 5$ AC Response Functions

AC Intercept	Calculation	Result
α_1	.4323 + 1.0952	1.5275
α_2	.4323 + .4365	.8688
α_3	.4323 + .5823	1.0146
α_4	.4323 + (−1.2670)	−.8347
α_5	.4323 − [1.0952 + .4365 + .5823 + (−1.2670)]	−.4147

In these expressions, the values in parentheses on the left side of the equations indicate the two adjacent categories being compared. These models can be used to find the predicted logits depending on *gender* for each response function; the predicted logits can then be transformed to estimate the odds and probability of being in the *higher* category out of the two adjacent categories indicated. The estimated response logits are provided in the final section of the printout, "Predicted Values for Response Functions." The observed logits are included in the first half of the table, so the estimated values can be compared easily to the actual values. For example, to calculate the predicted logit for males (*gender* = 1) in the 4th AC comparison (function 4 represents category 4 compared to category 3), we use the associated response model above: $\hat{Y}'(4,3) = -.8347 + (-.1928) \times gender = -.8347 + (-.1928) = -1.0275$. We can use this same process to find the corresponding predicted logit for girls (*gender* = 0): $\hat{Y}' = -.8347 + (-.1928) \times gender = -.8347$. If the predicted logits are exponentiated, the result is the odds of being in category 4 rather than category 3 for each *gender*. For boys, this is exp(−1.0275) = .3579, and for girls this is exp(−.8347) = .4340. Both boys and girls are less likely to be in category 4 rather than in category 3, similar to the findings of the CO and CR analyses. To calculate the odds ratio for boys to girls, we take .3579/.4340 = .8246, which is the exponentiated value for the effect of *gender* in the AC models, that is, exp(−.1928) = .8246. For all five AC response functions, the effect of *gender* is held constant with a corresponding common OR of .8246. Thus, according to the model, the odds for boys of being in the higher of two adjacent categories is .8246 times the odds for girls; boys are less likely to be in the higher proficiency categories for reading.

Actual frequencies and category probabilities for the proficiency by gender analysis were shown earlier in Chapter 4, Table 4.2 (first and second rows for the male and female sections of that table). The AC model does not predict the category probabilities; rather, the predictions obtained from the AC logit models can be used to estimate *conditional* probabilities for the higher response value of the two adjacent categories being compared. However, the predicted logits can be transformed to odds, and the odds can be transformed to predicted probabilities in the usual way: *p-hat* = odds/(1 + odds).

Using the data from Table 4.2 and the results of the AC model, observed and predicted AC probabilities were calculated and are provided in Table 6.2. Observed and estimated ORs also are included in Table 6.2. The probabilities are conditional on the specific adjacent categories being compared. For example, the first entry for males, .7725, represents the observed probability of a boy being in proficiency category 1 rather than the (next lower) adjacent category, proficiency level 0. This value is determined from the entries in Table 4.2 for these two adjacent categories: .7725 = 163/(48 + 163). The same value can be obtained by using the specific category probabilities from Table 4.2: .7725 = .0974/ (.0287 + .0974).

The predicted conditional probabilities from the AC model are shown in the bottom portion of Table 6.2. To determine the predicted probabilities from the logit models, we use the familiar expression $\hat{p}$ = exp(logit)/(1 + exp(logit)). For boys in comparison (4, 3), this becomes $\hat{p}_{4, \text{ males}}$ = .3579/(1 + .3579) = .2636, as shown in the fourth column, bottom portion, of Table 6.2. Similarly, for girls we have $\hat{p}_{4, \text{ females}}$ = .3026. These probabilities are conditional in the sense that they correspond only to the probability of being in the higher category, given response in either of two adjacent categories. Finally, it is evident from a visual comparison of observed to estimated odds ratios that a single value for the effect of *gender* across the AC categories seems to provide a parsimonious description of the data.

Overall, the model indicates that *gender* helps to explain differences in probability across adjacent proficiency categories. The *gender*-only model is an improvement over the null model, which does not fit the data:

TABLE 6.2
Observed (π_j^*) and Predicted ($\hat{p}_j^*$) Conditional AC Probabilities

AC Comparison	(1, 0)	(2, 1)	(3, 2)	(4, 3)	(5, 4)
$\pi_{j,\text{ males}}^*$	.7725	.6625	.6967	.2580	.3710
$\pi_{j,\text{ females}}^*$	.8582	.7043	.7316	.3071	.3836
OR (observed)	.5588	.8245	.8428	.7858	.9474
$\hat{p}_{j,\text{ males}}^*$	.7916	.6629	.6946	.2636	.3526
$\hat{p}_{j,\text{ females}}^*$	.8216	.7045	.7339	.3026	.3978
OR (estimated)	.8246	.8246	.8246	.8246	.8246

Residual chi-square for the empty model is $\chi^2_5 = 41.33, p < .0001$ (syntax D2, output not shown). Based on the *gender* model, we can conclude that boys are less likely than girls to be in the higher reading proficiency level of two adjacent categories.

Because the probabilities estimated from the model are conditional, and because each has a different base for comparison, there is no straightforward approach to estimating specific category probabilities for the AC model. Measures of association such as the τ_p and λ_p require these category probabilities for construction of the classification table. Agresti (1989) provides syntax and an example for calculating category frequencies based on adjustments to the baseline categories (multinomial) logit model and construction of a specific design matrix to constrain the slopes for an explanatory variable to be equal across AC response functions. This approach becomes quite complex as the number of explanatory variables increases and thus is not pursued here. However, there is a strong association between the actual and predicted probabilities from the AC model, Pearson's $r = .997$. This correlation is calculated for the two profiles (*gender*) across the five response models, so it is not surprising that the association is so high. As mentioned earlier, CATMOD uses weighted least squares rather than maximum likelihood to estimate the AC model; therefore, a likelihood ratio R^2 is not available for comparison with the previous two ordinal regression methods.

EXAMPLE 6.2: Adjacent Categories Model With Two Explanatory Variables

The CATMOD procedure is not designed to handle continuous explanatory variables, and estimation becomes problematic when unique covariate patterns have a small sample size within a data set. The full-model AC equivalent of the CO and CR models discussed previously was not estimable because of this limitation. The AC model can be fit through PROC GENMOD or SPSS GENLOG with adjustments from an unconstrained multinomial model, but those procedures differ somewhat from the regression approach presented in this book and thus are not considered here. Details on analysis of multinomial outcomes can be found in Agresti (1990, 1996), Allison (1999), Borooah (2002), Ishii-Kuntz (1994), and Tabachnick and Fidell (2001).

To illustrate a regression approach to AC analysis for a slightly more complex design, one of the continuous variables was selected, age at kindergarten entry (*plageent*), and a two-variable model (*plageent* together with *gender*) was developed. Following the method used by Clogg and Shihadeh (1994) for AC models with continuous predictors, age was grouped into four levels (*agecat*) representing a range of about 6 months each, starting at 57 months (4.75 years). Each of the explanatory variables (*gender* and *agecat*) was treated as quantitative through the "*direct*" sub-command (syntax D3).

The analysis generated eight covariate profiles, one for each of the 2 × 4 cross-classifications of the two explanatory variables. The sample sizes within the profiles ranged from 18 to 850. The residual chi-square test indicated a good fit for the model, $\chi^2_{33} = 30.49$, $p = .5929$. The slightly larger p value for the analysis suggests a small improvement over the *gender*-only model. Both *gender* ($\chi^2_1 = 42.06$, $p < .0001$) and *agecat* ($\chi^2_1 = 60.43$, $p < .0001$) were statistically significant in the model.

The five AC models are shown below. Intercepts for each model were determined following the same pattern as outlined in Table 6.1. The odds ratio for the gender effect is $\exp(-.2043) = .8152$, which is very similar to its effect in the previous *gender*-only analysis. Thus, controlling for age at kindergarten entry, boys are less likely than girls to be in the higher proficiency level of two adjacent proficiency categories. The odds ratio for the effect of age on proficiency is $\exp(.1607) = 1.1743$. Controlling for *gender*, older children are more likely to be in the higher proficiency categories for reading than younger children.

$$\hat{Y}'(1, 0) = 1.1373 + (-.2043) \times gender + (.1607) \times agecat$$

$$\hat{Y}'(2, 1) = .5544 + (-.2043) \times gender + (.1607) \times agecat$$

$$\hat{Y}'(3, 2) = .6871 + (-.2043) \times gender + (.1607) \times agecat$$

$$\hat{Y}'(4, 3) = -1.1718 + (-.2043) \times gender + (.1607) \times agecat$$

$$\hat{Y}'(5, 4) = -.767 + (-.2043) \times gender + (.1607) \times agecat$$

The assumption of parallelism in the effects of *gender* and *agecat* were verified through review of the underlying AC models corresponding to each response function (analysis not shown). For both explanatory variables, this assumption was plausible, given the logits and odds ratios derived for each model. The association between observed and predicted values was strong, with $r = .903$ for the eight profiles across the five response functions.

EXAMPLE 6.3: Full Adjacent Categories Model Analysis

To provide a comparison with results of the previous two chapters, the corresponding AC binary logistic regressions were run using the full set of predictors. Results are shown in Table 6.3. The odds ratios in bold print were found to be statistically different from 1.0. Results are fairly consistent with the findings of the CO and CR models in terms of direction of effects. In general, older children and children from higher SES families tend to be in higher proficiency categories for reading. Boys, children from families with defined risk factors (see Chapter 2), and, to some extent, children who attended only half-day rather than full-day kindergarten tend to be in the lower proficiency categories. Children who do not have books read to them frequently tend to be in lower proficiency categories, and the odds ratios for this variable are always less than 1.0, although this effect is not statistically significant in any of the AC models.

TABLE 6.3
Adjacent Category Binary Logits for the Full Models

Comparison	(1, 0) b (se(b)) OR	(2, 1) b (se(b)) OR	(3, 2) b (se(b)) OR	(4, 3) b (se(b)) OR	(5, 4) b (se(b)) OR
Intercept	4.10 (2.15)	−.34 (1.20)	−1.18 (.84)	−2.85** (.84)	−3.71** (1.21)
gender	−.64 (.31)	−.23 (.15)	−.26 (.10)	−.29 (.10)	−.12 (.14)
	.53*	.80	**.77****	**.75****	.89
famrisk	.19 (.33)	−.18 (.17)	−.09 (.11)	−.26 (.12)	−.02 (.18)
	1.21	.83	.91	**.77***	.98
center	.05 (.32)	−.24 (.17)	.18 (.11)	.00 (.12)	.20 (.19)
	1.06	.78	1.20	1.00	1.22
noreadbo	−.36 (.30)	−.13 (.18)	−.14 (.13)	−.07 (.15)	−.34 (.25)
	.70	.88	.87	.93	.72
minority	.28 (.33)	−.18 (.17)	−.41 (.11)	.17 (.11)	.16 (.16)
	1.32	.84	**.67****	1.19	1.17
halfdayK	−.07 (.30)	.10 (.15)	−.07 (.10)	−.30 (.10)	.13 (.14)
	.94	1.11	.94	**.74***	1.14
wksesl	.92 (.27)	.24 (.12)	.40 (.08)	.25 (.07)	.60 (.10)
	2.51**	1.27	**1.50****	**1.28****	**1.82****
plageent	−.03 (.03)	.03 (.02)	.036 (.01)	.03 (.01)	.04 (.02)
	.97	1.03	**1.04****	**1.03****	**1.04***
Model $\chi^2(df)$	22.75** (8)	20.17** (8)	97.61** (8)	44.27** (8)	56.58** (8)
H-L $\chi^2(df)$	7.36 (8)	7.25 (8)	12.70 (8)	5.40 (8)	9.40 (8)

*p < .05; **p < .01.

7. CONCLUSION

The purpose of this book is to illustrate the application of statistical techniques for the analysis of ordinal response variables and to familiarize applied researchers with methods for the analysis of ordinal data that are faithful to the actual level of measure of the outcome. Using data from the NCES's Early Childhood Longitudinal Study—Kindergarten Cohort (ECLS-K), three ordinal regression approaches were demonstrated: proportional or cumulative odds, continuation ratio, and adjacent categories models. In addition, variations on these models also were presented that allow for relaxed restrictions on the proportionality or parallelism assumption for some of the explanatory variables. The methods and examples illustrated here should enable researchers to apply similar models to their research data when their outcomes are in the form of ordinal responses.

The analysis of ordinal response variables requires a thoughtful and sensible strategy that should be guided more by the research question than by a desire to "fit" a particular model. There are many choices for analysis, and the most frequently used ordinal regression methods are covered here. The models identified above differ in terms of model predictions and interpretation of the effects of explanatory variables; thus, the choice between modeling approaches should always be guided by theory, either of how explanatory variables might affect the ordinal outcome or of how the ordinal scores were derived. Further, the choice should be guided by the purpose of a particular study as well as by the expected meaningfulness of results that would be obtained through application of a particular statistical model.

Cliff (1993, 1994, 1996b; Cliff & Keats, 2003) has been a consistent and strong proponent of the need to treat ordinal variables as ordinal, that is, to consider analyses of ordinal data that honor and preserve the processes through which those variables were actualized. His work has guided much of my own critical thinking regarding the use and analysis of ordinal outcome data. However, the goal of this work is not to advocate for a rigid adherence to methodologies based simply on the scale of a response variable. Rather, the goal is to further the understanding and use of ordinal techniques when the *ordinal* interpretation of the scores is of primary importance.

The analysis of ordinal mastery-type scores, such as the proficiency scale for early literacy developed from the ECLS-K data, holds great promise for attempts to understand why some children succeed at particular early-reading skills while others do not, and it can help researchers identify or develop interventions that are targeted toward improving individual proficiency depending on where the child is along the proficiency continuum. That is, the same intervention intended to move children from the lowest proficiency category to any higher proficiency may not be reasonable for children already in the two or three highest proficiency categories. The analysis of ordinal scores is similarly useful in other domains as well. For example, risk-reduction interventions, such as those developed to promote the consistent use of condoms, often have differential intervention messages that are targeted to people at a particular stage of readiness to change (Prochaska, DiClemente, et al., 1992; Stark et al., 1998). Thus, one size does not necessarily fit all in the context of ordinal outcome variables.

In the examples presented here, many similarities in direction of effects were observed. For example, first-grade children who have any family risk factors or who are not read to frequently by their parents or guardians are less likely than their peers to be in higher proficiency levels. Older first-grade children and those from families of higher socioeconomic status are more likely than their peers to be in higher proficiency categories. Reviewing the tables for the full-model CO and CR analyses, the odds ratios for all effects are directionally similar, but the interpretation of the odds ratio depends on the specific model constructed. Cumulative odds are designed to represent the odds of a child being at or beyond any particular proficiency category. Continuation ratios are designed to represent the odds of a child advancing beyond a particular category, given that the child has reached mastery in that category. Finally, the AC model is designed to estimate the odds of a child being in the higher category of two adjacent proficiency levels. An important question is "Which of these models is 'best'?"

The answer is simple: It depends on the research question. The CO model is useful if the focus of the study is on clarifying trends in the outcome, either upward or downward, for different values of the explanatory variables (Agresti, 1996). The CR model may be most useful in developmental-type studies, where identification of factors associated with being farther along on the response continuum, given that a certain stage has been reached, is of greatest interest to the researcher (O'Connell, 2000). The AC model can clarify which explanatory variables might best predict a response being in the next-highest response category, thus helping to identify differences between AC pairs of responses.

However, the "best" ordinal model will also be one for which assumptions of proportionality or parallelism are reasonable. Fitting and reviewing the corresponding binary models for each method, as was done here, can supplement available tests of these assumptions. Both the CO and the CR models can be adjusted to allow for interactions between the underlying cutpoints or divisions between categories; these are the partial proportional odds model and what can be called the partial proportional hazards model. Although both of these interaction models require a restructuring of the data set, these methods are enormously valuable in understanding differential effects of explanatory variables along the response continuum. For the ECLS-K study, the partial proportional hazards model might best represent the process of mastery and the factors associated with the likelihood that a child would actually attain mastery in a higher category.

Although the objective of the analysis of ordinal proficiency scores from the ECLS-K may support my preference in this particular case for continuation ratio models, no attempt is made here to position one ordinal regression alternative as more or less appropriate than another alternative. Each model imposes a different set of assumptions on the data and addresses a different kind of research question. It is incumbent on the researcher to fully understand the nature of these assumptions and how the decision to apply one model as opposed to another may affect the usefulness of a study's findings.

Assuming stronger measurement properties of the data than truly exist, such as treating ordinal outcome values as equal-interval scales, threatens to obscure the richness of patterns in the data that can be better brought to light through methods specifically designed for ordinal outcomes. Chapter 4 included a comparison of results for the cumulative odds model and the multiple linear regression model, and the results of that straightforward comparison should signal to researchers that a reliance on the familiar, such as a multiple regression analysis, can mask interpretation of important effects and lead to nonsensical predictions. On the other hand, ignoring the ordinality of the data completely and treating the outcome data as strictly nominal in nature hinders the ability to assess directionality and progression, which would seemingly have been the point of constructing an ordinal response measure in the first place. My hope is that using the work presented in this book, researchers will consider ordinal regression techniques among their analysis options, particularly when the research questions and the data indicate that such an approach is warranted.

Considerations for Further Study

In many ways, use of ordinal regression models is still an evolving methodology. I offer the following points of interest for those who wish to take the development and application of ordinal models further.

• The measures of association presented here, including τ_p, λ_p, and the likelihood ratio R^2 statistics, were very weak. This may be an artifact of the data; the distribution of proficiency was not balanced, and a large proportion of children at the beginning of first grade (44%) had attained mastery in proficiency level 3. Long (1997) points out that although summary measures of fit are desirable, "in practice they are problematic" (p. 102), as they provide only partial information about the quality of a model. Hosmer and Lemeshow (2000) present a compelling argument for why classification statistics from a logistic regression model are often inappropriate; one of these reasons is the tendency for classification to be driven strongly by the distribution of probabilities in the sample. Although their remark is specific to binary models, an extension to similar problems in classification for ordinal models is obvious. Nonetheless, studies that investigate the behavior of various measures of association for ordinal responses in different samples would provide valuable information to the field.

• Graphical methods for investigating the assumptions of proportionality or parallelism, as well as for residual diagnostics, are not well developed for ordinal methods. Neither SAS nor SPSS includes residual diagnostics embedded in its programs for ordinal regression (although both do for logistic regression). Although graphical and diagnostic techniques were not reviewed here, Bender and Benner (2000) present several diagnostic and graphical approaches for the subset of ordinal models that they consider.

• The analyses presented here assumed independence across individuals, and single-level models were fit to the data. However, the ECLS-K study is based on a multistage cluster sampling strategy, with children sampled from within sampled schools. Because the purpose of this study was to explicate the application of ordinal regression models, no adjustments for the multilevel structure of the data were included. Multilevel models for ordinal data are available through the major multilevel software packages, including HLM (Raudenbush, Bryk, Cheong, & Congdon, 2000), MLwiN (Goldstein et al., 1998), and MIXOR (Hedeker & Gibbons, 1996). HLM has capabilities to fit proportional odds models for multilevel data. MLwiN can fit proportional odds models and, with data restructuring, will estimate multilevel logistic continuation ratio models and logistic partial or nonproportional hazard models. MIXOR is designed specifically for multilevel analysis of ordinal outcomes, and it has more flexibility than either HLM or MLwiN. Link functions include logit, probit, and clog-log. Examples of multilevel ordinal models using the early literacy proficiency data from the ECLS-K study can be found in O'Connell, McCoach, Levitt, and Horner (2003).

NOTES

1. For further review of levels of measurement, refer to Cliff (1996b, chap. 1) and Agresti and Finlay (1997).

2. Information on access to the public-use ECLS-K data is available online at http://nces.ed.gov/ecls.

3. Revised proficiency scores were used (C1RRPRF1 to C1RRPRF5, etc.).

4. Proficiency levels in ECLS-K follow a Guttman model, such that students passing a particular skill level are assumed to have mastered all the lower skill levels. In the fall and spring first-grade data, only 5.5% of the children did not follow this pattern for reading and 6.6% did not follow this pattern for math. NCES (2002) reports that these patterns are probably more indicative of guessing than of a different order of skill acquisition for these students. In Grade 3 releases of the ECLS-K data, the highest proficiency score for each child as determined by NCES is now included directly on the database; earlier databases, including the one used in this book, contained only the dichotomous proficiency variables. For the small percentage of children whose response patterns do not follow the Guttman model, NCES reports their highest proficiency as "missing." However, for the data used here, I based the assignment of the ordinal proficiency score on a child's mastery (or not) of the highest skill level recorded in which three out of four items were answered correctly.

5. As one reviewer pointed out, it may be possible to conceptualize the ordinal scores derived through the ECLS-K as representing a count process, that is, a count of the number of proficiency categories passed by the student (0 to 5, for the first-grade ECLS-K data). Models for count data, such as the Poisson or the negative binomial, may be an alternative approach to the ordinal logistic models discussed in this book. There are, however, some limitations to those strategies for the ECLS-K data analyzed in this book, including the assumption of independence of events for a Poisson process, heterogeneity in the rate of mastery across students, and the upper limit on possible counts for the first-grade data. With the release of the third-grade data set, which expands the number of proficiency categories to 13 (including the original 0 to 5 proficiency categories), application of Poisson regression procedures may be an additional option toward understanding factors that affect children's learning. Those readers working with ordinal data that may be conceptualized better as resulting from a distinct counting process are referred to Long (1997), Allison (1999), or Liao (1994) for information on the development and application of Poisson regression procedures.

6. The discussion of deviance and the saturated model is somewhat simplified here. There are, in fact, several approaches to defining the saturated model, resulting in different values for the deviance. Interested readers are directed to Simonoff (1998) for details.

7. See Hosmer and Lemeshow (2000, pp. 147–156) for additional information related to the power of the H-L test, as well as for discussions of other tests of model fit.

8. As a measure of association, Somers' D has both asymmetric and symmetric forms. SAS PROC LOGISTIC computes and displays $D_{x.y}$ rather than $D_{y.x}$; that is, the predicted probabilities are treated as the dependent variable in the calculation of Somers' D. Space does not allow for detailed review of differences across forms of this statistic. Refer to Demaris (1992), Liebetrau (1983), Peng and Nichols (2003), and Peng and So (1998) for details.

9. SPSS performs a full likelihood ratio test rather than a score test for the assumption of proportional odds; the score test actually is an approximation to the full likelihood ratio test (D. Nichols, personal communication, 2004).

APPENDIX A: CHAPTER 3

The data and syntax for all analyses are available from the author and also can be located at the author's Web site at http://faculty.education.uconn .edu/epsy/aoconnell/index.htm. "Gonomiss" is the SAS data set with no missing observations for the subsample on the explanatory variables of interest. "ECLSFGsub" is the SPSS data set with no missing observations for the subsample on the explanatory variables of interest.

A1. SPSS LOGISTIC (for Proficiency Outcome 0, 1 Versus 5)

```
**  (cumsp2=0 if profread=0,1; else cumsp2=1 if profread=5).
temporary.
select if (profread le 1 OR profread eq 5).
logistic regression CUMSP2
  with GENDER
  /print=all
  /save=pred.
```

A2. SAS PROC LOGISTIC (Descending Option; Additional Options Shown)

```
**   data "go" contains only children with values of 0, 1, or 5 on
profread;
**   cumsp2 = 0 if profread=0,1 _ else cumsp2=1 if profread=5;
proc logistic data=go order=internal descending;
  model  cumsp2=gender  /link=logit  lackfit  ctable  pprob=.5001
    rsquare;
  output out=dataprobs pred=phat;
run;
```

A3. SAS PROC LOGISTIC (Default Is Ascending Option; Basic Options)

```
**   data "go" contains only children with values of 0, 1, or 5 on
profread;
**   cumsp2 = 0 if profread=0,1 _ else cumsp2=1 if profread=5;
proc logistic data=go order=internal;
 model cumsp2=gender /link=logit rsquare;
run;
```

A4. SPSS PLUM

```
temporary.
select if (profread le 1 OR profread eq 5).
PLUM
  cumsp2 BY gender
  /LINK = logit
  /PRINT = FIT PARAMETER SUMMARY TPARALLEL HISTORY(1) KERNEL
  /SAVE = ESTPROB PREDCAT PCPROB ACPROB.
```

APPENDIX B: CHAPTER 4

B1. SAS Ascending (CO Model), X1 = Gender

```
proc logistic data=sagebook.gonomiss;
  model profread =gender /link=logit rsquare;
  output out=propodds predprobs=cumulative;
  run;
```

B2. SAS Descending Option (CO Model), X1 = Gender

```
proc logistic data=gonomiss descending;
  model profread =gender /rsquare;
  output out=proppred predprobs=cumulative;
  run;
```

B3. SPSS PLUM (CO Model), X1 = Gender

```
filter by filt_$$.    ** filters out cases with missing data **.

PLUM
  profread  BY gender
  /LINK = LOGIT
  /PRINT = FIT PARAMETER SUMMARY TPARALLEL HISTORY(1) KERNEL
  /SAVE = ESTPROB PREDCAT PCPROB ACPROB .
```

B4. SAS Full-Model Cumulative Odds Model (Descending)

```
proc logistic data=sagebook.gonomiss descending;
   model profread =gender famrisk center noreadbo minority
     halfdayK
         wksesl p1ageent
         /link=logit rsquare;
   output out=proppred predprobs=cumulative;
   run;
```

B5. Partial Proportional Odds via SAS PROC GENMOD

```
**** CREATING RESTUCTURED DATA SET FOR THE PARTIAL PROPORTIONAL
ODDS ***;

data ppom; set gonomiss;
  do; if profread=5 then beyond=1;
  else beyond=0; split=5; output; end;
  do; if profread ge 4 then beyond=1;
  else beyond=0; split=4; output; end;
  do; if profread ge 3 then beyond =1;
  else beyond=0; split=3; output; end;
  do; if profread ge 2 then beyond=1;
  else beyond=0; split=2; output; end;
  do; if profread ge 1 then beyond=1;
  else beyond=0; split=1; output; end;
run;

proc freq data=ppom;
  tables split*profread*beyond;
  run;

proc sort data=ppom;
  by split gender famrisk center noreadbo minority halfdayK;
run;

** use INDEP structure, most similar to separate logit analyses;
** pg 541, Stokes, Davis, Koch (2000);

proc genmod descending order=data data=ppom;
  class split gender famrisk center noreadbo minority
    halfdayK childid;
  model beyond =gender famrisk center noreadbo minority
    halfdayK wkses1
        plageent split split*minority
    /link=logit d=b type3;
  repeated subject=childid /type=indep;
  run;
```

APPENDIX C: CHAPTER 5

C1. SAS: Restructuring the Data Set for Modeling *P*(beyond)

```
data cr1;
   set gonomiss;
   if profread ge 0;  crcp=0;       ** cont ratio cutpoint **;
   beyond=profread ge 1;            ** else = 0 **;
   run;


data cr2;
   set gonomiss;
   if profread ge 1;  crcp=1;
   beyond=profread ge 2;
   run;


data cr3;
   set gonomiss;
   if profread ge 2;  crcp=2;
    beyond=profread ge 3;
   run;


data cr4;
   set gonomiss;
   if profread ge 3;  crcp=3;
   beyond=profread ge 4;


data cr5;
   set gonomiss;
   if profread ge 4;  crcp=4;
   beyond=profread ge 5;
   run;


data concat;
   set cr1 cr2 cr3 cr4 cr5;
   if crcp=0 then dumcr0=1; else dumcr0=0;
   if crcp=1 then dumcr1=1; else dumcr1=0;
   if crcp=2 then dumcr2=1; else dumcr2=0;
   if crcp=3 then dumcr3=1; else dumcr3=0;
   run;
```

C2. SAS: Logit-Link CR Model With Descending Option

```
proc logistic data=concat descending;
  model beyond=dumcr0 dumcr1 dumcr2 dumcr3 gender /link=logit
     rsquare;
    output out=modC2 pred=phat;
run;
```

C3. SAS: Clog-Log Link CR Model With Ascending (Default) Option

```
proc logistic data=concat;
  model beyond=dumcr0 dumcr1 dumcr2 dumcr3 gender /link=cloglog
     rsquare;
    output out=modC3 pred=phat;
run;
```

C4. SAS: Clog-Log Link Cumulative CR Model With Ascending (Default) Option

```
proc logistic data=gonomiss;
  model profread=gender /link=cloglog rsquare;
  output out=modC4 pred=phat;
run;
```

C5. SPSS: Clog-Log Link Cumulative CR Model

```
PLUM
  profread  BY male
  /CRITERIA = CIN(95)  DELTA(0)  LCONVERGE(0)  MXITER(100)
    MXSTEP(5)
   PCONVERGE(1.0E-6) SINGULAR(1.0E-8)
  /LINK = cloglog
  /PRINT = FIT PARAMETER SUMMARY TPARALLEL HISTORY(1) KERNEL
  /SAVE = ESTPROB PREDCAT PCPROB ACPROB .
```

C6. SAS: Logistic CR, Full Model

```
**CR1 logit link;
proc logistic data=sagebook.concat descending;
  model beyond=dumcr0 dumcr1 dumcr2 dumcr3
          gender famrisk center noreadbo minority halfdayK
            wksesl p1ageent
    /link=logit rsquare;
  output out=modC6 pred=phat;
  run;
```

C7. SPSS: Cumulative CR, Full Model

```
PLUM
  profread  BY male famrisk center noreadbo minority halfdayk
   WITH
  plageent wksesl
  /CRITERIA  =  CIN(95)  DELTA(0)  LCONVERGE(0)  MXITER(100)
   MXSTEP(5)
  PCONVERGE(1.0E-6) SINGULAR(1.0E-8)
  /LINK = cloglog
  /PRINT = FIT PARAMETER SUMMARY TPARALLEL HISTORY(1) KERNEL
  /SAVE = ESTPROB PREDCAT (CRpred)PCPROB ACPROB .
```

C8. Creating a Classification Table in SPSS for Logistic CR Analysis Based on Model Estimates Obtained From Syntax C2 (SAS Descending)

```
*CR  Logit  Model  P(Beyond=1)  (Table  5.2)  gender  only
***********.
*Using Original Data set, n=3365 ******************.

compute int = -.3763.
compute dumcr0 = 4.4248.
compute dumcr1 = 2.9113.
compute dumcr2 = 1.9283.
compute dumcr3 = .0578.
compute slopegen = -.2865.


compute logit4 = int + slopegen*gender.
compute logit3 = int + dumcr3 + slopegen*gender.
compute logit2 = int + dumcr2 + slopegen*gender.
compute logit1 = int + dumcr1 + slopegen*gender.
compute logit0 = int + dumcr0 + slopegen*gender.


compute delta0=exp(logit0)/(1 + exp(logit0)).
compute delta1=exp(logit1)/(1 + exp(logit1)).
compute delta2=exp(logit2)/(1 + exp(logit2)).
compute delta3=exp(logit3)/(1 + exp(logit3)).
compute delta4=exp(logit4)/(1 + exp(logit4)).

*freq /var=delta0 delta1 delta2 delta3 delta4.

**   Now need complements of the deltas for the descending
logit link  ****.
```

```
compute compd0 = 1 - delta0.
compute compd1 = 1 - delta1.
compute compd2 = 1 - delta2.
compute compd3 = 1 - delta3.
compute compd4 = 1 - delta4.
compute compd5 = 1.0.

*freq /var=compd0 to compd5.

compute p0=compd0.
compute p1=compd1*(1-p0).
compute p2=compd2*(1-p0-p1).
compute p3=compd3*(1-p0-p1-p2).
compute p4=compd4*(1-p0-p1-p2-p3).
compute p5=compd5*(1-p0-p1-p2-p3-p4).

*freq /var=p0 to p5.

*****   now, take max category prob as choice for predicted
category.

compute maxphat=max(p0,p1,p2,p3,p4,p5).

compute predcls=99.
if (maxphat = p0) predcls=0.
if (maxphat = p1) predcls=1.
if (maxphat = p2) predcls=2.
if (maxphat = p3) predcls=3.
if (maxphat = p4) predcls=4.
if (maxphat = p5) predcls=5.

freq /var=predcls.

CROSSTABS
   /TABLES=profread BY predcls
   /cells=count expected
   /FORMAT=AVALUE TABLES.
```

98

APPENDIX D: CHAPTER 6

D1. AC Models

```
libname   sagebook   "C:\My  Documents\research\ordinal   new\
sagebook\ordinal sas stuff";

proc freq data=sagebook.gonomiss;
  tables p1ageent profread*gender;
run;

proc catmod data=sagebook.gonomiss;
  direct gender;
  response alogit out=acgender;
  model profread=_response_ gender /wls pred;
run;

proc contents data=acgender;
run;

data go; set acgender;
 odds=exp(_pred_);
 predprob=odds/(1 + odds);
 run;

proc freq data=go;
 tables gender*_number_*predprob;
 run;
```

D2. Null Model

```
proc catmod data=sagebook.gonomiss;
  population gender;
  response alogit out=nogender;
  model profread=_response_ /wls pred;
run;
```

D3. Two-Variable Model

```
data go2; set sagebook.gonomiss;
  if plageent le 62 then agecat=1;
  if plageent gt 62 AND plageent le 68 then agecat=2;
  if plageent gt 68 AND plageent le 74 then agecat=3;
  if plageent gt 74 then agecat=4;
run;

proc catmod data=go2;
  direct gender agecat;
  response alogit out=acfull;
  model profread=_response_ gender agecat /wls pred;
run;

proc contents data=acfull;
run;

data go3; set acfull;
 odds=exp(_pred_);
 predprob=odds/(1 + odds);
 obsodds=exp(_obs_);
 obsprob=obsodds/(1 + obsodds);
run;

proc corr data=go3;
 var obsprob predprob;
 var _obs_ _pred_;
run;
```

REFERENCES

AGRESTI, A. (1989). Tutorial on modeling ordered categorical response data. *Psychological Bulletin, 105*(2), 290–301.

AGRESTI, A. (1990). *Categorical data analysis.* New York: John Wiley & Sons.

AGRESTI, A. (1996). *An introduction to categorical data analysis.* New York: John Wiley & Sons.

AGRESTI, A., & FINLAY, B. (1997). *Statistical methods for the social sciences* (3rd ed.). Upper Saddle River, NJ: Prentice Hall.

ALLISON, P. D. (1995). *Survival analysis using SAS: A practical guide.* Cary, NC: SAS Institute.

ALLISON, P. D. (1999). *Logistic regression using the SAS system: Theory and application.* Cary, NC: SAS Institute.

ANANTH, C. V., & KLEINBAUM, D. G. (1997). Regression models for ordinal responses: A review of methods and applications. *International Journal of Epidemiology, 26*(6), 1323–1333.

ANDERSON, J. A. (1984). Regression and ordered categorical variables [with discussion]. *Journal of the Royal Statistical Society, Series B, 46,* 1–40.

ARMSTRONG, B. G., & SLOAN, M. (1989). Ordinal regression models for epidemiological data. *American Journal of Epidemiology, 129*(1), 191–204.

BENDER, R., & BENNER, A. (2000). Calculating ordinal regression models in SAS and S-Plus. *Biometrical Journal, 42*(6), 677–699.

BENDER, R., & GROUVEN, U. (1998). Using binary logistic regression models for ordinal data with non-proportional odds. *Journal of Clinical Epidemiology, 51*(10), 809–816.

BOROOAH, V. K. (2002). *Logit and probit: Ordered and multinomial models.* Thousand Oaks, CA: Sage.

BRANT, R. (1990). Assessing proportionality in the proportional odds model for ordinal logistic regression. *Biometrics, 46,* 1171–1178.

Center for the Improvement of Early Reading Achievement. (2001). *Put reading first: The research building blocks for teaching children to read, Kindergarten through grade 3.* Washington, DC: Government Printing Office.

CIZEK, G. J., & FITZGERALD, S. M. (1999). An introduction to logistic regression. *Measurement and Evaluation in Counseling and Development, 31,* 223–245.

CLIFF, N. (1993). What is and isn't measurement. In G. Keren & C. Lewis (Eds.), *A handbook for data analysis in the social and behavioral sciences: Methodological issues* (pp. 59–93). Hillsdale, NJ: Lawrence Erlbaum Associates.

CLIFF, N. (1994). Predicting ordinal relations. *British Journal of Mathematical and Statistical Psychology, 47,* 127–150.

CLIFF, N. (1996a). Answering ordinal questions with ordinal data using ordinal statistics. *Multivariate Behavioral Research, 3*(3), 331–350.

CLIFF, N. (1996b). *Ordinal methods for behavioral data analysis.* Mahwah, NJ: Lawrence Erlbaum Associates.

CLIFF, N., & KEATS, J. A. (2003). *Ordinal measurement in the behavioral sciences.* Mahwah, NJ: Lawrence Erlbaum Associates.

CLOGG, C. C., & SHIHADEH, E. S. (1994). *Statistical models for ordinal variables.* Thousand Oaks, CA: Sage.

COLE, S. R., & ANANTH, C. V. (2001). Regression models for unconstrained, partially or fully constrained continuation odds ratios. *International Journal of Epidemiology, 30,* 1379–1382.

101

COX, C. (1988). Multinomial regression models based on continuation ratios. *Statistics in Medicine, 7*, 435–441.

COX, D. R. (1972). Regression models and life tables [with discussion]. *Journal of the Royal Statistical Society B, 74*, 187–220.

DEMARIS, A. (1992). *Logit modeling* (Quantitative Applications in the Social Sciences, No. 86). Newbury Park, CA: Sage.

FOX, J. (1997). *Applied regression analysis, linear models, and related methods.* Thousand Oaks, CA: Sage.

GIBBONS, J. D. (1993). *Nonparametric measures of association* (Quantitative Applications in the Social Sciences, No. 91). Newbury Park, CA: Sage.

GOLDSTEIN, H., RASBASH, J., PLEWIS, I., DRAPER, D., BROWNE, W., YANG, M., et al. (1998). *A user's guide to MLwiN.* London: Multilevel Models Project, Institute of Education, University of London.

GOODMAN, L. A. (1979). Simple models for the analysis of association in cross-classifications having ordered categories. *Journal of the American Statistical Association, 74*, 537–552.

GOODMAN, L. A. (1983). The analysis of dependence in cross-classifications having ordered categories, using loglinear models for frequencies and log-linear models for odds. *Biometrics, 39*, 149–160.

GREENLAND, S. (1994). Alternative models for ordinal logistic regression. *Statistics in Medicine, 13*, 1665–1677.

GRISSOM, R. J. (1994). Statistical analysis of ordinal categorical status after therapy. *Journal of Consulting and Clinical Psychology, 62*(2), 281–284.

GUTTMAN, L. A. (1954). A new approach to factor analysis: The radix. In P. F. Lazarsfeld (Ed.), *Mathematical thinking in the social sciences* (pp. 258–348). New York: Columbia University Press.

HALL, G. E., & HORD, S. M. (1984). *Change in schools: Facilitating the process.* Albany: State University of New York Press.

HEDEKER, D., & GIBBONS, R. D. (1996). MIXOR: A computer program for mixed-effects ordinal regression analysis. *Computer Methods and Programs in Biomedicine, 49*, 57–176.

HEDEKER, D., & MERMELSTEIN, R. J. (1998). A multilevel thresholds of change model for analysis of stages of change data. *Multivariate Behavioral Research, 33*(4), 427–455.

HOSMER, D. W., & LEMESHOW, S. (1989). *Applied logistic regression.* New York: John Wiley & Sons.

HOSMER, D. W., & LEMESHOW, S. (2000). *Applied logistic regression* (2nd ed.). New York: John Wiley & Sons.

HUYNH, C. L. (2002, April). *Regression models of ordinal response data: Analytic methods and goodness-of-fit tests.* Paper presented at the annual meeting of the American Educational Research Association, New Orleans, LA.

ISHII-KUNTZ, M. (1994). *Ordinal log-linear models* (Quantitative Applications in the Social Sciences, No. 97). Thousand Oaks, CA: Sage.

JENNINGS, D. E. (1986). Judging inference adequacy in logistic regression. *Journal of the American Statistical Association, 81*, 471–476.

JOHNSON, R. A., & WICHERN, D. W. (1998). *Applied multivariate statistical analysis* (4th ed.). Upper Saddle River, NJ: Prentice Hall.

JÖRESKOG, K. G., & SÖRBOM, D. (1996). *LISREL 8 user's reference guide.* Chicago: Scientific Software International.

KNAPP, T. R. (1999). Focus on quantitative methods: The analysis of the data for two-way contingency tables. *Research in Nursing and Health, 22*, 263–268.

102

KOCH, G. G., AMARA, I. A., & SINGER, J. M. (1985). A two-stage procedure for the analysis of ordinal categorical data. In P. K. Sen (Ed.), *Biostatistics: Statistics in biomedical, public health and environmental sciences* (pp. 357–387). Amsterdam: North Holland.

KRANTZ, D. H., LUCE, R. D., SUPPES, P., & TVERSKY, A. (1971). *Foundations of measurement: Vol. I. Additive and polynomial representations.* New York: Academic Press.

LÄÄRÄ, E., & MATTHEWS, J. N. S. (1985). The equivalence of two models for ordinal data. *Biometrika, 72*(1), 206–207.

LIANG, K. Y., & ZEGER, S. L. (1986). Longitudinal data analysis using generalized linear models. *Biometrika, 73,* 13–22.

LIAO, T. F. (1994). *Interpreting probability models* (Quantitative Applications in the Social Sciences, No. 101). Thousand Oaks, CA: Sage.

LIEBETRAU, A. M. (1983). *Measures of association* (Quantitative Applications in the Social Sciences, No. 32). Beverly Hills, CA: Sage.

LONG, J. S. (1997). *Regression models for categorical and limited dependent variables.* Thousand Oaks, CA: Sage.

LONG, J. S., & FREESE, J. (2003). *Regression models for categorical dependent variables using STATA* (rev. ed.). College Station, TX: Stata.

McCULLAGH, P. (1980). Regression models with ordinal data [with discussion]. *Journal of the Royal Statistical Society, B, 42,* 109–142.

McCULLAGH, P., & NELDER, J. A. (1983). *Generalized linear models.* London: Chapman and Hall.

McCULLAGH, P., & NELDER, J. A. (1989). *Generalized linear models* (2nd ed.). London: Chapman and Hall/CRC Press.

McFADDEN, D. (1973). Conditional logit analysis of qualitative choice behavior. In P. Zarembka (Ed.), *Frontiers of econometrics* (pp. 105–142). New York: Academic Press.

MENARD, S. (1995). *Applied logistic regression analysis.* Thousand Oaks, CA: Sage.

MENARD, S. (2000). Coefficients of determination for multiple logistic regression analysis. *The American Statistician, 54*(1), 17–24.

National Center for Education Statistics. (2000). *America's kindergarteners.* Retrieved from www.nces.ed.gov/pubsearch/pubsinfo.asp?pubid=2000070

National Center for Education Statistics. (2002). *User's manual for the ECLS-K first grade public-use data files and electronic codebook.* Retrieved from www.nces.ed.gov/pubsearch/pubsinfo.asp?pubid=2002135

NESS, M. E. (1995). Methods, plainly speaking: Ordinal positions and scale values of probability terms as estimated by three methods. *Measurement and Evaluation in Counseling and Development, 28,* 152–161.

O'CONNELL, A. A. (2000). Methods for modeling ordinal outcome variables. *Measurement and Evaluation in Counseling and Development, 33*(3), 170–193.

O'CONNELL, A. A., McCOACH, D. B., LEVITT, H., & HORNER, S. (2003, April). *Modeling longitudinal ordinal response variables for educational data.* Paper presented at the 84th annual meeting of the American Educational Research Association, Chicago, IL.

PAMPEL, F. C. (2000). *Logistic regression: A primer.* Thousand Oaks, CA: Sage.

PENG, C. Y .J., & NICHOLS, R. N. (2003). Using multinomial logistic models to predict adolescent behavioral risk. *Journal of Modern Applied Statistical Methods, 2*(1), 1–13.

PENG, C. Y. J., & SO, T. S. H. (1998). If there is a will, there is a way: Getting around the defaults of PROC LOGISTIC. In *Proceedings of the MidWest SAS Users Group 1998 Conference* (pp. 243–252). Retrieved from http://php.indiana.edu/~tso/articles/mwsug98.pdf

PETERSON, B. L., & HARRELL, F. E. (1990). Partial proportional odds models for ordinal response variables. *Applied Statistics, 39*(3), 205–217.

PLOTNIKOFF, R., BLANCHARD, C., HOTZ, S., & RHODES, R. (2001). Validation of the decisional balance scales in the exercise domain from the transtheoretical model. *Measurement in Physical Education and Exercise Science, 5*(4), 191–206.

PROCHASKA, J. O., & DiCLEMENTE, C. C. (1983). Stages and processes of self-change of smoking: Toward an integrative model. *Journal of Consulting and Clinical Psychology, 51*(3), 390–395.

PROCHASKA, J.O., & DiCLEMENTE, C. C. (1986). Towards a comprehensive model of change. In W. R. Miller & N. Heather (Eds.), *Treating addictive behaviors: Processes of change* (pp. 3–27). New York: Plenum.

PROCHASKA, J. O., DICLEMENTE, C. C., & NORCROSS, J. C. (1992). In search of how people change: Applications to addictive behavior. *American Psychologist, 47*(9), 1102–1114.

RAUDENBUSH, S., BRYK, A., CHEONG, Y. F., & CONGDON, R. (2000). *HLM 5: Hierarchical linear and nonlinear modeling.* Lincolnwood, IL: Scientific Software International.

SIMONOFF, J. S. (1998). Logistic regression, categorical predictors, and goodness of fit: It depends on who you ask. *American Statistician, 52*(1), 10–14.

SINGER, J. D., & WILLETT, J. B. (2003). *Applied longitudinal data analysis: Modeling change and event occurrence.* New York: Oxford University Press.

SNOW, C. E., BURNS, M. S., & GRIFFIN, P. (Eds.). (1998). *Preventing reading difficulties in young children.* Washington, DC: National Academy Press.

STARK, M. J., TESSELAAR, H. M., O'CONNELL, A. A., PERSON, B., GALAVOTTI, C., COHEN, A., et al. (1998). Psychosocial factors associated with the stages of change for condom use among women at risk for HIV/STDs: Implications for intervention development. *Journal of Consulting and Clinical Psychology, 66*(6), 967–978.

Statistical Analysis System. (1997). *SAS/STAT software: Changes and enhancements through release 6.12.* Cary, NC: Author.

Statistical Analysis System. (1999). *SAS Onlinedoc Version 8.* Retrieved from http://v8doc.sas.com/sashtml/

STEVENS, S. S. (1946). On the theory of scales of measurement. *Science, 103*(2684), 677–680.

STEVENS, S. S. (1951). Mathematics, measurement, and psychophysics. In S. S. Stevens (Ed.), *Handbook of experimental psychology* (pp. 1–49). New York: Wiley.

STOKES, M. E., DAVIS, C. S., & KOCH, G. G. (2000). *Categorical analysis using the SAS System* (2nd ed.). Cary, NC: SAS Institute.

TABACHNICK, B. G., & FIDELL, L. S. (2001). *Using multivariate statistics* (4th ed). Boston: Allyn & Bacon.

VAN DEN BERG, R., SLEEGERS, P., GEIJSEL, F., & VANDENBERGHE, R. (2000). Implementation of an innovation: Meeting the concerns of teachers. *Studies in Educational Evaluation, 26*, 331–350.

WEST, J., DENTON, K., & GERMINO-HAUSKEN, E. (2000). *America's kindergarteners: Findings from the early childhood longitudinal study, kindergarten class of 1998-99: Fall 1998* (NCES 2000-070). Washington, DC: U.S. Department of Education, National Center for Education Statistics.

ZILL, N., & WEST, J. (2001). *Entering kindergarten: A portrait of American children when they begin school* (NCES 2001-035). Washington, DC: National Center for Education Statistics.

INDEX

ABOUT THE AUTHOR

Ann A. O'Connell is Associate Professor of Educational Psychology at the University of Connecticut, Storrs, where she is also the coordinator of the graduate program in measurement, evaluation, and assessment. She teaches graduate-level statistics and educational research methods including multi-level modeling, logistic regression, sampling and survey research methods, multivariate analysis, and introductory statistics. Her collection of published work focuses, in general, on research applications using these and other advanced statistical/research techniques, primarily in the areas of HIV prevention, program evaluation, and the analysis of large-scale databases such as the ECLS-K. She has also published on methods of teaching to improve learning in applied statistics courses. Her work has appeared in journals including *Women and Health, Evaluation and the Health Professions, Measurement and Research in Counseling and Development, Morbidity and Mortality Weekly Report (MMWR),* and *Journal of Educational Research.*